A beginner's guide to planning for trading success

Trading Plans made simple

Jacqueline & Davin Clarke

Wrightbooks

First published 2011 by Wrightbooks
an imprint of John Wiley & Sons Australia, Ltd
42 McDougall Street, Milton Qld 4064
Office also in Melbourne
Typeset in Berkeley LT 11.5/13.4 pt
© Jacqueline Clarke 2011
The moral rights of the author have been asserted
National Library of Australia Cataloguing-in-Publication entry

Author:	Clarke, Jacqueline.
Title:	Trading plans made simple: a beginner's guide to planning for trading success / Jacqueline Clarke; contributor, Davin Clarke.
ISBN:	9780730375401 (pbk.)
Notes:	Includes index.
Subjects:	Speculation.
	Stocks.
Other Authors/Contributors:	Clarke, Davin.
Dewey Number:	332.64

Cover images and design by Peter Reardon, Pipeline Design <www.pipelinedesign.com.au>

Printed in China by Printplus Limited

10 9 8 7 6 5 4 3 2 1

Disclaimer

The material in this publication is of the nature of general comment only, and does not represent professional advice. It is not intended to provide specific guidance for particular circumstances and it should not be relied on as the basis for any decision to take action or not take action on any matter which it covers. Readers should obtain professional advice where appropriate, before making any such decision. To the maximum extent permitted by law, the authors and publisher disclaim all responsibility and liability to any person, arising directly or indirectly from any person taking or not taking action based upon the information in this publication.

Contents

About the authors

Jacqueline Clarke is a trader and a chartered accountant with extensive experience in senior finance roles for various businesses. She has a keen understanding of the importance of planning for any financial endeavour and the impact planning has on the success rate of any business activity. She has over 10 years' experience in trading as a business. As a trader and accountant, Jacqueline has an understanding of both business and trading, providing a unique perspective for this book.

Davin Clarke is principal of Tzar Corp and is a successful full-time private trader. Davin has earned his primary income from trading since 2000, and has a first-hand understanding of what it takes to trade full time. Davin provides a limited number of high-level trading skills workshops through Tzar Corp for futures and options traders. Davin is regularly sought for speaking engagements and is featured in a number of books, including *The Wiley Trading Guide* published by John Wiley & Sons, *20 Most Common Trading Mistakes and How You Can Avoid Them* published by Wrightbooks and *Real Traders, Real Money, Real Lives* also published by Wrightbooks.

Acknowledgements

We have been very fortunate to have worked with a great team of people in writing this book. Our thanks and appreciation to John Wiley & Sons Australia, and in particular Kristen Hammond for her enthusiasm, support and advice, and to Michael Hanrahan for his fantastic editing skills and attention to detail.

To all our clients and the many traders we have had the pleasure of knowing, we thank you for providing us with the opportunity to work with you and see you grow as traders. You have provided much of the inspiration for us to produce this book.

chapter 1

Planning to succeed

The scope of this book

Trading Plans Made Simple is designed to provide you with a guide to building a comprehensive plan for your personal trading. When we mention trading, we are referring to anyone who actively manages his or her investments for the purposes of generating income, short-term profits or longer term capital gains. Many of you may consider yourself investors and believe that a trading plan is not suitable for you. Wrong! We strongly urge everyone who is serious about generating a return from their trading or investing to ensure they have a comprehensive plan for success.

We will guide you through the entire process, from setting your goals, evaluating your resources, evaluating what to trade, understanding risk, managing your trades and different types of strategies to measuring your success. In the final chapters we will show you how to bring together all of these elements to create a personalised trading plan tailor-made for you.

Throughout this book there are many exercises that you need to complete in the development of your trading plan. To assist you with this, we have created an online resource that you can use to complete these exercises and create your personal trading plan. Each exercise in this book is numbered so that you can easily find the reference in the online template. Simply go to <www.tzarcorp.com>.

The purpose of this book

The purpose of this book is to not only motivate and inspire you to achieve trading success but to also provide a framework for realising that success. Our objective is for you to have a clear picture of what you want to achieve from your trading and a detailed plan on how to achieve those goals. The only way to do that is to create a trading plan that is tailor-made for you. Your trading plan must take into account your personal goals, your personality, your strengths and your resources. For these reasons, it is important for you to work through all the chapters. Some chapters or parts of chapters may not appear to be important or particularly relevant to you; however, if you persist you will see how all the parts come together to provide the information you need for your trading plan.

A personalised and comprehensive trading plan is as equally important for an experienced trader as for a beginner. We have written this book in such a way that beginners, or those who are relatively new to trading, can effectively create a trading plan at the outset. However, this book is also an invaluable resource for any experienced trader who may wish to review and improve his or her trading, or who is currently trading without a trading plan. In fact, we have had many experienced traders who have worked through this book comment that it was a fantastic process for them to create focus and discipline in their trading (and consider a number of issues they hadn't thought of!).

The more you put into working through the information and exercises contained in this book, the better your plan will be. When reading through the chapters, think carefully about your answers to each of the exercises. Try to be honest and candid in your responses.

This plan is for *you*, so make sure you treat it with care and respect. Some chapters you may find more difficult to work through, particularly when examining yourself, looking at your goals, and evaluating your personal strengths and weaknesses. If you can be honest, accurate and comprehensive with your answers, your efforts will be greatly rewarded. You will be able to approach your trading with clarity and focus using a trading plan that is custom designed for you.

Tip

The best trading plan for you is one that is designed around you!

Why have a trading plan?

Just as every business needs a robust plan for success, so too does your trading. Throughout this book we will show you how to plan for your own success. At the end of this book you will be able to visualise your goals, understand what your commitment will be and determine your plan of action.

We encourage you to treat your trading and investment as a business, so that you apply the same level of discipline and attention to your trading as you would give to any business you manage. What we are really talking about is managing your money, and ensuring you generate a return from your money that is commensurate with the risk you take. Without a trading plan, you haven't defined the returns you want or the risk you are prepared to take in order to achieve those returns. You certainly wouldn't invest in any other business without understanding what your inherent risks and potential returns are. Trading should be no different to any other business. Whether you choose to trade long term, short term, full time or part time, the same business principles need to be applied to ensure success and maximise your returns.

Your trading plan will provide you with structure and an action plan for every aspect of your trading. Trading can be a highly emotional activity so a trading plan that sets out your response to any number of trading situations will guide you to make the correct decision at the critical time. Instead of flying by the seat of your pants you will have a well-considered plan of action. Making decisions based on feelings of panic and fear or overconfidence and greed is more likely to result in poor trading outcomes. Your trading plan will assist you to work through the times of stress like a professional.

In trading you cannot control the market—that is one of the elements of trading that makes it so exciting on the one hand but potentially stressful on the other. What you can, and must, control is yourself. Your trading plan will help to give you that control.

It is generally well accepted throughout the business community that having clearly defined goals is a key element to personal and business success. In working through this book you will be asked to examine your reasons for trading and define your trading goals. Thus, a trading plan will provide you with clear goals and the motivation to implement your plan in order to achieve those goals.

Your trading plan will also assist you to review and improve your results. Each of your trading strategies will be set out in your trading plan. Within the plan will be actions to review your results, benchmark and assess your strategies, and look for areas for improvement. If you don't have a plan to start with, you have little chance of assessing if it is working or how to make it better.

Tip

Trading plans give you the control to trade like a professional. If you fail to plan, you plan to fail.

Trading plans and discipline

One of the key attributes to success in trading is discipline. In fact, a key attribute to success in almost any field is discipline.

Discipline takes on many facets, particularly in relation to trading. We would like to discuss each of these facets in turn, and show you the importance of your trading plan in fostering and developing this discipline. After all, it will be a key to your success. Following are the facets:

⇨ Trading requires discipline to ensure you undertake the necessary investment in your own knowledge and education to attain an appropriate level of expertise. It is tempting to take the easy road and rely on news, gut feel or even tips. However, this will not provide you with a path to long-term success. You must develop the discipline to take the time and effort required to invest in your own financial education so that you develop the skills and knowledge to trade successfully. Development of your trading plan will identify any areas of learning that you need to address, and will help you schedule the time and create a process in order to attain this education.

⇨ Trading requires discipline in management of your trading account. You need to be rigorous in the development and application of your trading strategies. Develop detailed plans for identification of each trade, and a detailed action plan for all market outcomes. Disciplined application of these plans will be essential to your success. The process of developing these plans will foster an emotional investment and ownership of your own strategies, helping you to develop the discipline to follow through with those plans.

⇨ Trading also requires a high degree of self-management. Trading can be a highly charged and emotional activity. Any number of emotions can threaten to influence your actions. Feelings of elation and greed when trades are successful and feelings of fear and despair when trades are unsuccessful can threaten your trading success. These emotions can cause you to take actions that result in poor trading outcomes. A trading plan without the self-discipline to implement and follow it is not much better than no plan at all. However, the good news is that going through the process of creating a trading plan helps you to foster that discipline. A systematic approach that examines all aspects of your trading will subconsciously reinforce the importance of this plan. The effort and detail you put in as you work through this guide will create an emotional buy-in to your decisions and assist you to take the time and effort to ensure its implementation.

Tip

Trading requires discipline in both management of your account and your own self-management.

An individual approach

Aside from discipline, another important element in trading success is to have an individual approach that suits you, your personality and your lifestyle. One of the great things about becoming a successful trader is that there is no one formula for success. There are many very successful traders and investors throughout the world, all of whom approach their trading in different ways. This is one of the elements of trading that makes it so enticing.

There are successful long-term investors, who select their positions based on detailed fundamental reviews, right through to successful intraday traders who enter trades based on technical chart analysis only. There are successful equities traders, foreign exchange traders and derivatives traders.

Some would-be traders believe that all they need to do is follow a trading system. Unfortunately, there are many trading systems available in the marketplace but even more traders who fail to make consistent profits in the market. Having a trading system that does not suit your trading style is unlikely to provide you with long-term trading success.

This is why it is so important to develop your own personal trading plan and why we feel so passionate about this book. This is a fantastic tool for you to develop a trading approach that is perfectly suited to you: your skills, your personality, your goals and your lifestyle.

Ordinary people from many walks of life have achieved great things because they set their goals, created a successful plan and had the passion to follow through. This book provides the structure and guidance for you to set your goals and create your own personalised trading plan.

Trading can provide a fantastic lifestyle plus personal and financial success. You just need to be prepared to define your goals, take an individual approach, apply discipline in all aspects of your trading and possess a genuine passion and enjoyment for trading.

Chapter summary

⇨ Planning is essential to the success of any business. Treat your trading as a business and create a comprehensive plan for trading success.

⇨ Your trading plan must take into account your personal goals, your personality, your strengths and your resources. The best trading plan is one that is designed around you.

⇨ A trading plan is equally important for new traders as it is for experienced traders.

⇨ A trading plan will provide you with structure and an action plan for every aspect of your trading.

⇨ One of the key elements to success in trading is discipline. Discipline is needed to put in the work required to gain the skills and knowledge to become a successful trader.

⇨ Discipline is required to effectively manage your trading account and every aspect of executing your trading strategies.

⇨ Self-discipline is especially important in trading to control your actions in the face of a wide array of conflicting emotions.

⇨ Spending the time to develop a trading plan, and the plan itself, are both excellent tools to instil and foster the discipline you need for trading.

chapter 2

Defining
your goals

In this chapter we will work with you to explore and define your goals and reasons for trading. In any endeavour in life you undertake you are far more likely to achieve success if you have clearly defined goals. Not only do we want you to have clear goals for your trading, we want you to have a picture of what your overall financial and lifestyle goals are, and link these to your trading. Creating a picture of what your life can be and how trading will help you get there will provide strong motivation to succeed.

Why do you want to be a trader?

Why do you want to be a trader? This might seem an obvious question, and most people answer that they simply want to make lots of money. However, answering 'to make money' is not enough. It requires effort, skill and discipline to become a consistently profitable trader for the long term. You need to invest time in both your education and the development of your skills. As a result, you need a good reason to devote your time and energy in this way. The reasons for wanting to be a trader need to be well defined, personal and specific. Trading is not something to be undertaken lightly. It is a business with an inherent level of risk and a significant failure rate.

A vital but often dismissed aspect of all successful traders is passion. They are passionate about what they do and look forward to their trading activities with a sense of anticipation and excitement. During the time that you are building your trading business, you will experience many highs and lows. You will have times that are stressful and upsetting, and other times when you experience jubilation and a sense of achievement. A passion for trading will help you to ride through all of these. In particular, your passion will allow you to approach setbacks as a challenge and an opportunity to improve. To do this your passion for trading needs to be tied to your goals. You need to define, understand and believe in your goals to ensure losses do not dampen your enthusiasm or cause your confidence to falter.

Tip

A passion for trading will keep you focused and energised to trade well and be successful, and clearly defined goals will help to harness a passion for trading in order to achieve those goals.

It is an important step to understand what you want to achieve from your trading business. Why do you *want* to be a trader? Many people assume that it is simply to make money. However, it is not just the money we want. It is what money can buy us that we really desire. For some people these are material things, for others it may be travel, for others it may be more time or the option to stop working. Focusing on these things helps you to create and foster your motivation to succeed.

Goal setting

For some people, the process of goal setting can be a difficult one. It may take some time for you to discover what it is that you really want to achieve. It will require you to be very honest with yourself and to have courage to own and commit to your goal. Your objectives will most likely contain some financial element, but to succeed over the long term you need more than just a financial reward. What are your personal reasons? What burning desire do you hold that can be achieved, or you can move closer to, through trading? What is it you really want that money can buy you? Let us give you some examples:

⇨ Is it a need to be self-sufficient, and to generate an income to replace your existing salary?

⇨ Do you have a desire to be your own boss?

⇨ Does trading provide an outlet for your own personal development to learn new skills?

⇨ Do you crave a sense of achievement that you don't get from your current career?

⇨ Do you want to provide more for your family?

⇨ Do you want to live on the beach and drive a BMW?

⇨ Do you want to be able to travel and experience other places and cultures?

⇨ Do you want to grow your wealth to have more time and lifestyle choices?

⇨ Do you love the thrill and challenge the markets provide?

These are important considerations that will help you determine your trading strategy and trading time frame. Your short-term goals may be to supplement your income to build your wealth over time so that you can buy the house and car you desire. This will involve a very different approach to trading compared to someone whose passion is to be a successful, professional, full-time trader.

Your goals must come with an emotional attachment or a burning desire. Visualise what it will be like when you have achieved your goals. Put up pictures that encapsulate the things you want or the lifestyle you want. It might be a house, a car, a boat or faraway places. Think about what will change in your life. What do you receive, and how does it feel? Setting your goals this way allows you to harness your passion and will help you to stay focused and diligent.

Tip

We don't really want to make money to have the actual money. It is what money can buy us that we are really after. And it is also not just material possessions that money can buy. It is often time, flexibility or experiences that we can gain.

When writing down your goals, ensure they are specific and contain a time frame. Don't just write, 'I want to be a millionaire'. *When* do you want to be a millionaire? *How* do you want to have made the money? *What* is it that you think being a millionaire will bring you? What do you *really want* that being a millionaire will bring you (rather than just being a millionaire)?

Think BIG

Don't be afraid to think big. It's just as easy to set a large goal as a small one, so be careful not to place limits on what you can achieve. Every large goal can be broken down into smaller, more manageable targets for you to work toward. In chapter 7, we will be setting specific trading goals on short-term time frames that will move you toward this longer term goal. You will feel motivated and energised by a goal that challenges and excites you, so ensure your goal is, in fact, challenging and exciting to you.

Believe

Believe in your goals. It is best to write your goals down to affirm them in your mind. Put them up where you can see them. This may be a written statement you see each day at your desk, or a picture of what your goal represents where you can see it every day. Keep repeating your goal to yourself because you believe that it is possible and achievable.

Where are you now?

The place we will start in setting your goals is to look at where you are now. This provides you with a benchmark for moving forward. This is where we start to work on your trading plan by working though the activities outlined in this book. You can write your answers in a journal that you can use as you work through all the exercises, or you can use the online template we have developed which you can access from <www.tzarcorp.com>.

Tip

You need a concept of where you are now, plus where you want to be, before you plan the journey.

 Activity 2.1

Define your current situation. A clear picture of your current situation will help you see what you want to change and define your goals for the future. Where are you now? What is your current situation? Think about your life in terms of your wealth, income and lifestyle balance. What do you like about your life now? What do you want to change? Write down your answer

For example: I am working full time at the bank and earn $45 000, but I do not enjoy going to work. I have to travel 45 minutes to and from work each day. We have a nice home with a mortgage. I drive a Honda. I enjoy where I live and am interested in the stock market. I don't feel we have enough money to travel often and pay off the house at the same time.

Activity 2.2

Where do you want to be? Can you see and feel what it will be like when you are a successful and professional trader? What material things do you really want? Will you work? What is your work and lifestyle balance like? What does your typical day look like? Where do you live? What do you drive? Write down your answers or use pictures to help you define the lifestyle you want. Or use a combination of both. Find pictures from magazines of the things you want, and write about what your days will consist of. It is a great idea to involve your partner if you have one as he or she needs to understand and support your goals, and vice versa.

Some people can answer these questions immediately. Others need some time to examine their life and what is really important to them. In answering, consider your wealth, health, family and lifestyle in addition to material possessions. Be really specific in your responses. If using pictures, get a large piece of cardboard and create an inspiration board for your goals.

> For example: In seven years' time I want to build my net assets to $2 000 000. I will drive a BMW and live in a large modern house near the beach. I want to have enough income to travel overseas each year. I will work four days a week and have one day at home to devote to managing my trading business. I will have time to coach my son's football team, and I will go to the gym three times a week and feel great.

Some of you may be thinking that your goal is just too far away and too big to be real enough for you. If you have set yourself a big goal, it may be useful to break this down into smaller goals based along a shorter term time frame. You need to believe that you can achieve your goals. To do this, create some interim goals to aim for on the journey to your ultimate lifestyle. As you reach each of your smaller goals on your journey, your ultimate goal will start to appear all that much closer and more achievable.

So now that you have a clear picture of where you are now and where you want to be (your long-term goal), we need to link this picture to your trading. How will trading help you get there? Do you want trading to change your life in the short term, or are you trading to build your wealth for the longer term? Or more likely it is a mix of both. Having a very clear idea of what you want to do with the profits from your trading will help you to focus on achieving those results and ensure you apply those profits in accordance with your plans.

 Activity 2.3

Consider how trading is going to help you achieve the long-term goal you have outlined. Also consider how trading may impact your life on a shorter term time frame. Once again, it is important to be clear and specific in your response.

> For example: I will save 50 per cent of all profits from my trading to invest long term to build my wealth. This saving will be added to my current repayments to reduce and eliminate the mortgage on my home in the next four years. Thereafter, I will continue to use 50 per cent of all profits toward building my wealth to achieve my long-term goals. The other 50 per cent I will use to improve my current lifestyle. In the short term I will use this for travel to Vietnam next year. When this 50 per cent profit allows, I will reduce my work days from full time to four days—my goal is to achieve this within two years.

As you can see, there is some time and effort required to really define what you want from life, both now, in the next few years and in the longer term. We urge you to really spend some time on this, to create a very clear picture of exactly where you want to be. If you know where you are now and where you want to be, developing the plan on how to get there is the easy part. If you don't know where you want to be and it doesn't really mean anything to you, then your goal is just a number. It is much harder to maintain your motivation and enthusiasm for a goal that you don't really own.

Tip

When you are managing the profits from your trading, ensure you 'keep your eye on the prize'. Always keep in mind what your goals are and keep striving to achieve them.

Are you prepared to work hard enough to achieve your goals? This is an interesting and crucial question. Many people say they want to be rich but are not prepared to put in the effort (or maybe they just don't have clearly defined and personal goals to work toward!). If you are not prepared to work hard, perhaps you need to re-evaluate what you really want.

Activity 2.4

On a scale of 1 to 10, where 1 is impossible and 10 is easily achievable, rate how achievable you think your long-term goals are. Do you really believe that you can achieve them?

| 1 | 2 | 3 | 4 | 5 | 6 | 7 | 8 | 9 | 10 |

Impossible   Achievable

Activity 2.5

On a scale of 1 to 10, where 1 is no effort and 10 is 100%, rate how much effort you are prepared to put in to achieve your goals. Are you *really* prepared to work hard and invest your time and effort to achieve your dream lifestyle?

| 1 | 2 | 3 | 4 | 5 | 6 | 7 | 8 | 9 | 10 |

No effort   100% effort

If your answer to activity 2.4 is below 3 or above 8, perhaps you need to re-evaluate your goals. If you believe them to be impossible it is likely that you won't achieve them. This is not to say that you couldn't achieve them, but not believing that you can is a very large barrier to overcome.

Also consider your answer to activity 2.5 in the same way. If your answer is less than 7 you need to consider why this is the case. If you are not committed to achieving your goals, are they what you really want?

Reviewing your goals

Reviewing your goals is a crucial part of any process of growth and achievement. It is important to review your goals for a number of reasons. Your circumstances may have changed and had an impact on what is important to you. For example, health issues are often a significant driver of change in people's lives. Family is another significant factor affecting a person's goals. A second reason for reviewing your goals is to assess how much you have achieved and recognise those achievements. It is great for your motivation and confidence to recognise your success. A third reason is to refocus and set new goals that continue to challenge and excite you.

So review your goals regularly. For some people this occurs every day in the form of a to-do list that contains individual tasks that lead to their goal. Every day you can write down one thing that you will do to help achieve your goals. This is a simple and effective way to ensure you allocate some time for you and your goals. It is very easy to set some goals and then become so busy in your daily life that you find you don't have time left over for them. To avoid this trap, put your goals first. Ensure your immediate list of things to do includes at least one action that will help you toward achievement of your goals.

For others, reviewing their goals is a weekly, monthly or annual event. Some people feel strongly that if they spend the time determining their goals and commit them to paper, then they have enough ownership and focus that subconsciously they will work toward them over a longer time frame. And this is great.

We recommend you have a mixture of all of these: a daily or weekly to-do list, short-term targets for each trading session (however you wish to define this) and a periodic review of how your short-term goals are moving you toward your overall goals.

Tip

How often you review your goals will be closely tied to the time frame over which your goals are set. Annual goals need to be reviewed at least annually. In addition, you can review progress of your goals monthly or weekly.

✎ Activity 2.6

Determine how often you will review your goals. Consider your personality and ability to remain focused on your goals. What time frame will you use to set your goals, and how often will you spend time to review and acknowledge your achievements so far, reassess what is most important to you and reset your goals for the next period? Will you review your progress on a shorter time frame? Will you write down one thing that you will do to help you achieve your goals every day or every week?

For example: I have set my ultimate lifestyle goals to be achieved over the next eight years. In working toward this, I have set annual goals that move me toward this goal. Each year, I will review and assess my achievements and reset new goals for the next year. I will have my goals displayed on my office wall and use a diary in which I will record one action to complete each week that will help me achieve my annual goals.

Chapter summary

⇨ To become a successful trader over the long term you will need to have clearly defined goals and harness your passion for trading.

⇨ Successful traders really enjoy their trading. They know why they are traders and what they want to achieve from trading.

⇨ It is important for you to understand why you want to be a trader and what you want to achieve from it.

⇨ Goals are more effective when they are personal and emotive. Goals in terms of lifestyle (for example, what possessions you can afford, your ability to travel, where you live) are far more powerful and motivating than purely financial goals.

⇨ Writing down your goals and using pictures to help define them is a wonderful process to help you define what is really important to you.

⇨ When writing down your goals, be specific and include a time frame.

⇨ Don't be afraid to think big! Large goals can always be broken down into smaller objectives.

⇨ You need to believe that your goals are achievable to make the investment of your time and energy to reach them. You also need goals that are challenging and exciting to you.

⇨ Assessing the level of effort you are prepared to put in to achieve your goals will highlight if the goals you have set are the right ones for you.

⇨ Reviewing your goals is important to recognise your success, reassess if your circumstances (and hence your goals) may have changed and set some new goals for the next period.

⇨ A simple to-do list can be a powerful tool for you to achieve your goals. If you simply include one action each day or each week that you will undertake to help you achieve your goals, you will be amazed at how much you can achieve.

chapter 3

The business of trading

Trading in financial markets is a business. In this chapter we will show you how approaching your trading in a businesslike manner will greatly increase your efficiency and your profitability. In this chapter, you will work through a number of exercises to determine your business assets, many of which revolve around you, your knowledge and skills, and the resources you have available.

Your approach to trading

Regardless of your individual trading strategy, the market you trade or your time frame, trading, like any other business, must be approached with a high level of professionalism.

An arbitrary and unsystematic approach that is 'hit or miss' is likely to provide you with inconsistent results and is far more likely to result in losses. Even if it is occasionally successful it will not provide sustainable returns for you in the long run. Assuming that your goal for trading is to create a business generating a sustainable profit over time, your chances of successfully achieving that goal are greatly increased through creating your own plan.

As in any business, planning is a key contributor to your ongoing success. Think of this as a business plan for your trading. You wouldn't embark upon running any other business without a business plan, and your trading business should be given the same level of effort and discipline.

The results you achieve when you approach your trading as a business will not rely on luck. They will be the outcome of your hard work and planning; the result of setting goals, obtaining the right business assets, creating a plan and implementing that plan.

Why do so many fail?

You have probably heard market commentators remark that anecdotally only somewhere between 5 per cent and 20 per cent of traders actually make money. Well, why do so many fail in this particular business?

One reason is often the failure to apply a businesslike approach to trading. If you go into trading saying to yourself, 'I will start with $20 000 because that is what I can afford to lose', then you will probably lose your $20 000. This unprofessional approach has no goal, no structure and little chance of success. In fact, subconsciously you are already accepting that you are going to lose. That is not to say that you should put everything you have into your trading account. Part of your business planning is to ascertain how much capital you can place at risk given your personal circumstances. Your level of trading capital will be an objective and considered decision, a decision made with a view to creating a long-term profitable business—not a gamble that if it doesn't work it doesn't matter.

Tip

Your state of mind and the way in which you think about trading will impact upon your trading success. If you believe you are unlikely to win, then you probably won't. If you believe you are building a business to generate wealth and long-term profits, then you are far more likely to succeed.

Your approach to trading should be with a view to creating a successful business. However, we do make one exception to this rule: if, when working through chapter 2, you identified that your goals in trading were really tied to enjoying trading as a pastime for some fun, then your view of trading will be different. And that is perfectly valid if that is what you want. You just need to know how much you wish to spend on that activity and enjoy!

Your business plan

Your business plan is designed to ensure you are fully aware of all the variables and parameters under which you will be operating your trading business. This includes an understanding of your goals, your resources, your expected returns and your expenses. It also includes an analysis of all the things that might go wrong, and having a predetermined plan of action for when they do! This is called your disaster recovery plan — and every business should have one.

Part of your business plan will include your trading strategy plan, which will detail your trading strategies and the markets you will trade. We will cover this later. Now that you understand your reasons for trading and have set yourself some broad goals for your trading, you need to start on your business plan. In this part of your business plan you will consider some of the less exciting, but still equally important, aspects of becoming a successful trader.

Steps you need to complete for your business plan include:

1   Determine your trading resources.

2   Understand yourself and your personal approach
     to trading.

3   Calculate your setup and operating costs.

4   Build your trading strategy plan.

In this chapter we will be guiding you through the first step to determine your trading resources. Your trading resources include your personal knowledge and skills as well as the physical assets that you need to operate your trading business. As you work through this book we will cover each of the steps listed above.

Your aim is to develop a comprehensive plan to create a successful trading business that suits you. Don't be scared of the word *business*. Our use of the word business does not imply that this has to be a full-time activity for you. Your trading business has to suit you and your lifestyle. It may be a long-term approach that can be managed part time. Or you may wish to trade every day. Either way, we strongly urge you to approach your trading as a business with a well-thought-out plan—your chances of success will be greatly increased. Importantly, your plan will be designed around your personality, your skills and your lifestyle.

Tip

Your trading business does not need to be a full-time business. Your business needs to suit you, your skills, your goals and your lifestyle.

Establishing your trading business

There are four elements we have identified that you need for successful trading:

⇨   the appropriate knowledge and skills

⇨   appropriate resources

⇨ a business plan

⇨ a trading strategy plan.

Let's consider knowledge and skills first. You will need to build your knowledge and skills over a number of areas. Of course, you will need to build knowledge and skills directly related to trading; however, you will also need to build knowledge around the operation of the market, the use of brokers and software, and some general accounting and record-keeping skills, just to name a few.

The resources you need for your trading business will include some physical assets as well as services from third parties, such as brokers, software and internet access. You also need to evaluate your personal resources and attributes that will impact upon your trading success. Trading is a very individual activity that is highly dependent upon you and your actions. This is often referred to as your trading psychology. It will be important for you to understand your personal attributes and natural tendencies, and how they will impact upon your trading.

When referring to your business plan, we are talking about all the processes that you need to consider that surround the actual execution of your trades. These include activities such as time management, risk management and disaster recovery. We also include your trading strategy plan (that is, your specific plans for your trading strategies and execution of your trades) within your overall trading business plan.

We will work through each of these elements together as you work through this chapter and the rest of this book.

Knowledge and skills

For every trade on the market, there is a buyer and a seller. And the buyer and the seller have a different perception of where the market is going to move next. The buyer believes the price is going to go up, and the seller believes the price is going to go down.

When you start trading, remember that there is someone else at the other end of your trade. This person disagrees with your decision to buy or sell, and is taking the *exact opposite* position.

And who do you think this person is? You will be taking positions against the likes of:

⇨ professional traders with large bank accounts

⇨ stock brokers with vast resources for research and training

⇨ experienced fund managers

⇨ if you're really lucky, the average punter!

You are placing yourself, and your money, into the market to compete with these players. They are all trying to take your money and make a profit for themselves. So don't treat it lightly. Treat your trading like a serious business.

Activity 3.1

Think about the following question carefully.

Would you trust your money to another person to trade for you, who has the same level of knowledge and experience that you do?

This is a confronting question for most people. People readily accept that they can make trading decisions with their own money, but are far more cautious when considering allowing someone else to risk their money on the market. What we would like you to do is critically evaluate the trading knowledge and skills you currently possess and determine where you should invest in your education.

As we have already stated, you need to obtain the appropriate knowledge and skills for trading. The key word in this phrase is 'and'. Knowledge of how to trade is not the same as gaining the skills of trading. Knowledge encompasses an understanding of markets, market analysis, financial instruments, trading strategies, trade management, risk management and the like. All of this knowledge can be obtained through self-study, mentoring or courses. However, the skills of trading encompass the ability to apply this knowledge in an effective manner in *real* time into the *real* market to make a *real* profit. In trading, the application of knowledge, or trading skill, is always more difficult than the theory. The skills of trading can only be gained through *experience*.

Trading knowledge

Trading knowledge can be acquired from a number of avenues. The best teachers are usually those who actually trade and have a number of years experience with profitable trading. They will have been through the process you are about to undertake and have already learned from their mistakes. However, these traders can be difficult to find and it is often difficult to assess how much someone really trades. If considering learning from someone or undertaking a course, try to find independent testimonials and comments from other traders who have been through the education program you are considering. The internet is a great place to start your research, with numerous trading blogs that are active and informative. Trading clubs are also a great source of information about what other traders have learned, what they have found useful and what they would recommend. There are also a variety of books on trading and a plethora of free information and articles on the internet for you to choose from.

Tip

Trading clubs and blogs can be a great source of support and a great network of like-minded people. They can also be a terrific source of information on not only course providers but on brokers, software and all things trading.

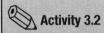 **Activity 3.2**

List your trading *knowledge* strengths and weaknesses. This will include your general knowledge about markets, financial instruments, software, brokers, executing trades, trade analysis, trade management, risk management, position sizing and trading strategies. For the areas in which you need to improve, set some goals and an action plan for addressing these.

Trading knowledge: strengths

List your trading knowledge strengths.

For example: I have a good understanding of the stock market and am comfortable with my knowledge about shares. I have studied charting and chart patterns, and feel I understand basic technical analysis skills to identify support, resistance and trends. I am confident with downloading data into my charting software, and can filter and analyse the shares to identify trading opportunities. I understand trade management in relation to my trading strategy.

Trading knowledge: weaknesses and action plan

List your trading knowledge weaknesses and a strategy for improvement. Be specific and set time frames.

For example: I am not sure of the best way to exit my trades, nor confident about how many shares I should buy (position sizing). I would also like to expand my technical knowledge and learn more about market structure and price analysis.

Strategy: Research courses available from traders who use price analysis and market structure to find a suitable course by the end of next month. Check trading blogs for feedback from other people who have done the course. Join a trading blog to build knowledge, and spend 30 minutes a week reading relevant comments. Read a technical trading book every three months.

For example: I would like to generate an income from options but need to learn more.

Strategy: Research and enrol in an options course by December. Do the same research into the provider as for technical analysis above. Read the book *Trading Options* this month.

Trading skills

Knowing what to do and actually being able to do it are two very different things. There is nothing quite like actually putting your own money into the market. You will experience a range of emotions: fear, excitement, greed, elation, devastation. Understanding how you react, and controlling those emotions and reactions (or even lack of action), is a key to your success.

Trading experience will help you gain the skills you need to implement your trading plan with as little emotion as possible. This experience will ensure you execute your trades in accordance with your plans and don't hesitate or panic. Inexperienced traders often enter trades in accordance with their well-planned trading strategies, only to exit poorly or not exit when they should as emotions overtake them. This is often the direct result of a lack of experience, and hence a lack of trading skill.

Experience will add to your understanding of the market, so that you will start to become familiar with the ways in which particular markets or securities behave and mould your trading strategies appropriately. As you become more experienced you will also recognise patterns and opportunities more rapidly. This will add to your ability to execute trading decisions with precision and confidence.

 Activity 3.3

List your trading *skills* strengths and weaknesses. Your trading skills will include skills such as speed of trade execution, ability to recognise patterns in real time, ability to navigate your broker's platform and ability to follow your trading plan. If you haven't started trading yet, that's okay. We look at some of the skills you may have that can be applied to trading in chapter 4.

Trading skills: strengths
List your trading skills strengths.

For example: I always enter according to my trading strategy plan. I can readily recognise my entry criteria and always enter based on my entry trigger.

Activity 3.3 *(cont'd)*

Or: I have been trading for a few years and I am very comfortable using the entry tools with ABC Broker.

Trading skills: weaknesses and action plan

List your trading skills weaknesses and a strategy for improvement. Be specific and set time frames.

For example: Although I enter well, I let my losses blow out and don't stick to my stops, hoping not to take a loss.

Strategy: I will keep detailed records and focus just on stops for the next 20 trades. I will record how I am feeling during the trade and why I did or did not follow my stops.

For example: I am new to trading and have just set up an account with ABC Broker. I am not very quick using the trade entry screens.

Strategy: I will set up a simulation account and practise entering and exiting trades until I am efficient at using the broker software.

If you are new to trading, when you start to take positions in the market remember to start slowly. Start with a small number of small positions. This will allow you to manage your portfolio more easily, and a smaller percentage of your capital will be at risk. You will start to build your trading skills with each trade that you execute. As you gain experience, you can increase the number of positions you hold and the size of your positions. You will start to feel when you have too much to manage and it will become stressful for you. Recognise when you are reacting due to emotions such as fear and stress rather than systematically applying your trading plan. Learn to read and acknowledge this, and reduce your positions accordingly until you build up your experience and skill.

Tip

Successful traders all started at the beginning. They had to build their knowledge and skills through education, practise and experience.

Appropriate resources

Trading does not require a significant investment in assets and staff, unlike many other businesses. And for many that is part of the reason they are attracted to trading as a means to generate assets and income. However, there are a number of resources that you will need to become a trader. Perhaps you may not have considered some of these at the outset; but, now you can make an informed decision on the resources you require, the resources you have and those you may need to invest in.

We like to categorise the resources you will need to be an effective trader into four areas:

⇨ time

⇨ financial

⇨ physical assets

⇨ personal attributes.

We will have a look at the first three resources before we examine your personal attributes in more detail in chapter 4.

Time

Let's talk about time first. The amount of time you set aside for trading will affect how long it will take you to build your knowledge and skills, as well as impact upon a number of aspects of your trading strategy. When you are new to trading, allocate time to invest in your trading education. You need time to attend that course, read that book, review those trading blogs, attend a traders' meeting and so on. It will be difficult for you to build your knowledge while managing the other competing interests in your life if you do not make trading one of your priorities and plan for time that you will spend on your trading education. Consider this time an investment in your future. The more time you spend now (and perhaps the less time in front of the television), the faster you will be generating a return from trading.

The time you have available for trading (once you are ready to start trading) will also impact upon the trading strategy or strategies you will use. For instance, you cannot hope to be an intraday trader if you are working full time and can only trade a few hours at night. You may aspire to be a full-time trader when you have built up your knowledge and your skills; however, for now you need to work within your current constraints. One option to build your intraday trading skills while working full time may be to intraday trade an overseas market that operates at times you are not working. You can trade for a few hours on an intraday basis in this market to build your trading skills.

You will also need to allow time for preparation and review. These are very important steps which can be easily overlooked when you are pressured for time. Preparation is important to ensure you have a sound view of all the factors that will impact your trading decisions before you actually enter any trades. You do not want to experience any nasty surprises after you enter a trade. For example, consider that you have entered a position in a stock for a swing trade you expect to last for about two weeks. The stock met your entry criteria and you have placed an automatic stop with your broker (often referred to as a contingent order; this is an order to exit your trade if the price falls to a certain level). Everything is looking great so far. However, on day four the stock drops dramatically in price, your stop is triggered and you are automatically sold out of the stock. What you didn't know is that the stock went ex-dividend on that day and as a result the price has adjusted down by the approximate amount of the dividend. You have exited the trade for no good reason!

If trading stocks, you will also need preparation time to enable you to filter and review the stocks available to select the trading opportunities best suited to your trading strategy.

Not allowing time for these important steps will reduce your profit potential both immediately and over time.

Time is also required for review. An essential part of building any knowledge or skill is to continually measure your outcomes and determine where you need to focus on improvement. Reviewing your trades will involve recording details of your trades and assessing the success of both the execution of your trading strategy and the success of the actual trading strategy itself. It is important to know whether your trading strategy works so that you can continue to use it, or whether it requires some adjustments. However, critical to this analysis is also knowing how effectively and accurately you implemented that strategy. The strategy may be fine but you are not achieving positive results as your execution is poor. Or conversely, your execution may be perfect but your strategy is flawed. It is important for you to know which one it is so you can take the most appropriate action. We will be exploring various ways in which to measure and assess your results in chapter 7.

Tip

Your current level of knowledge and experience will have an impact on the amount of time you will need to allocate to your trading. Like anything, the more time you spend on your trading, the faster it will grow and develop.

Sounds like trading will take up a lot of your time? Not necessarily. We are not suggesting that each of these tasks needs to be performed every day and take up a significant amount of time. The time you will need and frequency with which you do your learning, preparation and review will depend upon your current level of trading knowledge and your particular trading style and trading strategies. For example, an intraday trader will need to spend time on preparation every morning before the market opens. However, a long-term position trader may only undertake preparation and review on a weekly or even monthly basis.

 Activity 3.4

Complete the following questions to determine the time you have available and how you will allocate this time for your trading. This will assist in the development of your trading plan and strategies. Some of these questions you may wish to revisit after you have determined more of your trading plan and trading strategies.

How much time per day/week/month do you have to devote to trading? (This is uninterrupted time to concentrate and actually trade, but need not be all at the same time.)

For example: The time I will allocate to trading will be as follows:

- two hours each Sunday night
- one hour on Tuesday and Thursday nights after work
- half an hour each other weeknight
- extra time on Saturday for study and reading.

How much time will be spent on preparation? When will you do this?

For example: I will spend one hour each Sunday on trade preparation for the week ahead. This will include setting my trading goals for the week, performing a scan to filter potential stocks for trading, reviewing the overall market, filtering stocks to determine if they fit my strategy, checking for any announcements or dividend dates, and reviewing all open positions.

How much time will be spent on furthering your trading education? When will you do this?

For example: I will spend one hour each Friday night or Saturday (whichever fits best) on my trading education. This will include reading articles posted on <Trade4Edge.com> and reading a current technical book on market price analysis.

An important step for traders is to record and review all their trades. You need to objectively review your decisions and results to find your strengths and identify areas you need to improve. How much time will you spend on review? When?

For example: I will spend one hour each Sunday prior to my weekly preparation for review of my week's trading. This will include reviewing each of my trades and the notes taken, checking charts to ensure the trades were in line with my strategy, identifying areas in which I need to improve and including these in my goals for the following week.

Once you have scheduled your time for preparation, education and review, you also need to schedule the times when you will actually enter and monitor your trades.

For example: I will spend half an hour each weeknight to enter my orders based on my entry criteria. During this time, I will also monitor all current positions to determine if I need to adjust my stops or exit the trade.

Financial resources

There are two aspects to consider when talking about your financial resources. These are capital and income.

Capital

Capital is the amount of funds you have available for trading. It is the value of your account before you make any trading profits and the money that you put at risk in order to generate a trading profit. As a new trader, it would be unwise to commit all your available funds, or capital, to trading until you have a sound trading strategy and have developed your skills and expertise. Your trading capital is one of your most precious resources so you need to protect it. If you lose your trading capital, you greatly diminish (or even extinguish altogether) your ability to keep trading. So consider how much capital you are willing to commit to your trading business during your learning process. Then consider how much capital you will have when you are an established trader.

Your capital will play a key role in the development of your trading plan. It will influence the type of market and instruments you will trade. For example, if you are starting out with a small amount of capital, you will not be able to effectively trade high-value stocks and may choose to trade stocks with a lower price or use a leveraged instrument such as a contract for difference (CFD). The size of the trading account will also determine your risk level for each trade and your position size (this is covered in chapter 8).

Income

Income is the next financial consideration. Income is the money you need to generate on a regular basis to cover your daily needs, expenses and lifestyle. Income from trading tends to vary over time, as every trade will be different and all traders experience losses at some time. In fact, losses are a normal part of trading and just need to be managed within your trading plan. Particularly when starting out as a trader, consider your income requirements. Do you have other income sources you can rely on as you learn to trade?

Is your goal to replace your current income or supplement your current income? Consider also the amount you wish to earn from trading. You may wish to review your answers to activities in chapter 2 when considering this question. How does this income level compare to the level of capital you wish to commit to trading? The following activity will help you to work through these questions.

Tip

If you are planning to replace your current income with trading profits, you will need to have an alternative income source until you build the trading skills required to generate consistent profits at the level you desire. As a beginner, relying on your trading profits to pay the mortgage will place a huge amount of stress on you and may affect your trading decisions.

Activity 3.5

How much capital do you have for trading? What percentage of your available capital will you commit to trading now?

> For example: I aim to have $50 000 in my trading account once I feel that I have built the skills and experience to trade this amount. I will start my trading account with $25 000 as I am learning — for the next six months. Once I have achieved consistent results over a two-month period, I will increase my capital to $40 000, and similarly to $50 000.

Do you wish to borrow funds or use leverage to increase your trading capital? If so, how much? How will you do this (for example, derivatives or a margin loan)?

> For example: My current trading capital is $20 000 and I wish to have a trading account closer to $100 000. As I will be end-of-day trading over a medium to long-term timeframe, I will open a margin account to achieve the capital base with which to trade. I will ensure I include an analysis of my current borrowings, loan-to-valuation ratio and risk in my weekly review and preparation to allow enough available equity in my account to cover usual market price variations in the stocks I will be holding.

How much do you wish to earn from your trading? This can be a percentage or a dollar amount per week, month or year. Put a time frame on your target. You may even consider setting targets for the short term and the longer term.

> For example: I wish to replace my current income of $50 000 per year with trading income by the end of the second year.

> Or: I wish to earn 2 per cent a month of my capital from my trading. My current capital is $40 000, so I will try to return $800 per month.

Based on the previous few questions, calculate the percentage return you need to achieve your desired income from your capital. Is this realistic? Do you need to revisit the previous question?

> For example: I wish to earn $50 000 per year from trading, and my current trading capital is $25 000. This would be a 200 per cent

Activity 3.5 *(cont'd)*

return! In light of this, I will utilise a margin loan facility to increase my available capital to approximately $80 000. I will then aim to earn 2 per cent per month and retain the profits until I reach my goal of $50 000 per annum (after interest costs from the margin loan).

Do you have other income sources to support you while you are learning to trade? If so, how much?

For example: I will continue in my current job while I am trading so I am not reliant upon my trading profits for daily living costs. Trading profits will be invested for my future wealth and to supplement my current income.

Physical assets

Your physical environment for trading is also important. You need to be comfortable and able to concentrate fully. Remember that we are approaching this endeavour in a businesslike way. This means ensuring you have an office or a separate quiet area for trading. A comfortable chair and a desk are important, plus somewhere to file your records and paperwork in an orderly fashion. Trying to trade with a laptop on your knee and the television in the background is neither appropriate nor productive. You wouldn't try to operate any other business like this, so don't treat your trading this way.

Apart from furniture and space, you primary investment in physical assets will be computer equipment. You will also need other items for your trading. You may need additional hardware such as a modem and/or router to connect to the internet. A firewall is also a consideration to protect you and your computer while you are connected to the internet.

The internet

Although your internet connection is not a physical asset, we would like to add a few points on this now. There are a variety of means by which you can connect to the internet, and most of you will already be familiar with these and most probably already have the internet connected at your home. Internet reliability and speed can have an impact on your trading, so you need to review your current internet connection to ensure it will meet your trading needs. For most end-of-day traders, internet speed is unlikely to be a big issue; however, it will impact upon the time it will take to load your broker software, enter trades and stops, and download data for charting. For short-term traders, the reliability and speed of your internet connection will be far more significant. An unreliable connection can cost you dearly if trading opportunities are missed or stops are not executed because the internet dropped out. Your internet speed will also impact the time it takes for your orders to reach your broker and therefore the exchange, potentially affecting your execution price if there is a delay.

Tip

Regardless of how you connect to the internet (wireless, cable, ADSL), ensure your internet connection is protected from unauthorised users. Password protection on your internet connection, particularly if you have a wireless connection, is an easy and effective way in which to achieve this.

Computer equipment

The type of trading you will be doing may also impact the computer equipment you invest in. If you are planning to be an active intraday trader over a wide range of stocks, you may consider utilising multiple screens, in which case you will need a compatible graphics card in your computer. Intraday traders may also consider investing in a uninterruptible power supply (UPS). With such a short-term focus, it is important to remain online and able to manage your positions. A UPS will ensure that if there is a power interruption or failure at your house, your computer and internet will continue to operate for some time using a battery backup. Perform an analysis on the equipment you need to stay on in the event of a power failure and ensure the UPS you use has the capacity to run this equipment over a suitable time for you.

Tip

If investing in a UPS, ensure you have it set up correctly. Ensure your modem, computer and screens are all connected via the UPS. Without each of these connected, you may as well not have the UPS at all.

This may sound all very technical and confusing. Don't worry—you don't need to be a computer expert to be a great trader. You just need to talk to a local computer expert and ask the right questions. Ask friends and family to recommend someone who can help you with the information and equipment you need.

There are a few other items of equipment you may wish to consider. An external hard drive may be useful if you wish to back up your data on a separate drive in case of hardware failure. A printer will also be an item to consider. Documents you may wish to print include your trading records and charts for your trading review, your current short-term trading goals (we cover this in chapter 7) and your results. Some people prefer to have all these documents on their computer and can easily use them this way; for others a hard copy is more effective.

Software

The final topic we wish to discuss in this section is software. The range of trading software available is mind boggling, and it can be difficult to determine what you need or even what it is that you want. The software you buy will be entirely dependent upon your trading style, so we urge you to consider your software needs after you have completed the section on your trading style.

Charting software packages are only effective if they have price data on which to operate, so consider where you will access your data from and when it will be available. Many brokers provide delayed end-of-day data free of charge, which can be sufficient. Many traders prefer to use a data supplier to gain more current data, or have data that is adjusted to smooth out certain corporate events such as dividends and share splits. Intraday traders will need reliable and fast live data feeds for trading.

Tip

The cost of your data will increase with the speed and reliability of your data feed, as well as the volume of data (the type of data and the number of markets it covers) you need. Try not to fall into the trap of paying for data that you do not need for your trading strategy.

We will discuss the process for evaluating and selecting your trading partners in chapter 5. Your trading partners include your broker, educator/training provider, and software and data providers.

Activity 3.6

Complete the following questions to determine the assets you have currently and if you need to upgrade or purchase additional items for your trading.

Do you have your own computer? Is this equipment good enough to operate efficiently for online trading? When is it available for trading?

For example: We have a computer at home that has enough speed and data storage for trading. Based on my time schedule,

---

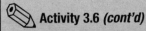 **Activity 3.6** *(cont'd)*

my family is aware of when I require the computer to be available for my trading and I do not need a separate computer.

Do you have an office or quiet area in which to work and file your documents? Do you have a comfortable chair and desk at which to work? When is it available for trading?

For example: We have an office at home with a suitable desk and filing cabinet. My chair is broken and uncomfortable so I will need to invest in a new one so that I can concentrate on my trading while working in the office. As my family also shares the office, I have advised them of my trading schedule so that the office is available to me at those times.

Do you have internet access which is uninterrupted during your trading times?

For example: Our current internet speed is ADSL2+ and our connection has been reliable to date. This will meet my trading needs.

Risk assessment and disaster recovery

Trading has been our family's sole source of income for the past eight years, so this topic is dear to our hearts. We can assure you that if you trade over any significant period of time, you will discover (as we have!) that things can go wrong. If you haven't planned for it then it can cost you a lot of time, stress and money. This is particularly so for intraday traders like ourselves; we are very dependent upon our equipment and services while trading.

The extent to which you plan for 'disasters' will be driven by your level of trading and your trading style. That is why we called this section risk assessment and disaster recovery. You need to firstly assess the risks and their potential impact, and then determine if you need to create and invest in a backup solution.

The risks we are referring to are those that impact your ability to operate your trading business in an effective manner. We are not talking about the inherent risk for any particular trade—this is discussed later in chapter 8 on money management.

We will discuss some of the more common risks to your trading business and suggest some potential ways in which to plan for these risks. It is not possible for us to outline the 'best' solution, as the best solution will be different for everyone depending on their trading style, level of risk tolerance and the amount they want to spend on mitigating these risks.

In the following exercise we will ask you to consider a number of different trading risks and present a number of alternative suggestions.

Tip

If you do not plan for these events, all of which are more than probable, then you certainly will have a plan after it has happened to you!

It can be very costly, particularly for a short-term trader, to lose access to your trading data and positions, even for a short time. Don't be caught rummaging through the phonebook trying to find the number of your broker; a little planning can save you the stress and potentially a lot of money.

✎ Activity 3.7

Consider the following scenarios and determine the impact on your trading and any actions you will take to offset the risk.

What will you do if the power is unavailable due to an unexpected outage?

Suggestions:

- Intraday traders: Invest in a suitable UPS and ensure it is properly connected to my computer, modem and screen.

Activity 3.7 *(cont'd)*

- Longer term traders: Have my broker's phone numbers written down and taped to the wall and also in my wallet so I can phone to execute any urgent orders. I can also phone to check the status of any orders I was entering when the power went out so I know if they were successful or not.

What will you do if the power is unavailable for several hours due to line maintenance in your area?

Suggestions:

- Intraday traders: Take the day off! Use the time to read a new trading book.

- Intraday traders: I can use the computer and my laptop at a relative's/friend's home for the day.

- Longer term traders: No issue. I am at work during the day so no impact on my trading.

What will you do if the internet is unavailable due to an unexpected outage?

Suggestions:

- Intraday traders: I have a backup wireless internet setup on my laptop so I can switch to that to see the status of my trades. I can use the laptop to execute trades if required or use the phone to contact my broker.

What will you do if your computer hardware (or modem) fails?

Suggestions:

- I have a backup laptop that I can use in an emergency. I also have a great relationship with a computer supplier and repairer who will be able to fix the problem or supply me with a new machine fairly quickly.

- I back up my data weekly, along with all my charts and trading records, on an external drive. Any data lost for part of a week can be easily reconstructed and I can download the price data again without charge.

What will you do if the batteries in your wireless keyboard or mouse go flat and you can't operate the computer?

Suggestions:

- Intraday traders: I always have spare AA and AAA batteries for the keyboard and mouse in my top drawer.

- Other traders: I usually have spares, but can run down to the shop if need be.

These are some of the events that may affect your trading in a negative way. Some may not seem a big issue for you; however, let us assure you it will be a big issue if something happens mid-trade and you end up losing money as a result!

Tip

Create a list with all your critical service providers' details, including your account name, account number and their phone numbers. This will be very handy if you lose power or connectivity at any time—and is just really handy while you are trading anyway!

Chapter summary

⇨ Approaching your trading as a business in a businesslike manner will greatly increase your chances of success.

⇨ The word 'business' encompasses your view of your trading—it does not mean it needs to be a full-time endeavour.

⇨ Like any business, planning is a key determinant of success.

⇨ Your trading business plan will ensure you consider all the parameters and variables likely to affect your trading, and provide you with a plan of action for most events.

⇨ Trading requires both knowledge and skill.

⇨ Knowledge can be gained from study; however, trading skills can only be gained from experience.

⇨ It is valuable to critically evaluate your current level of trading knowledge and trading skills to identify your strengths and weaknesses and create a strategy to improve.

⇨ When you are new to trading, remember to start slowly until you build up both your trading knowledge and trading skills.

⇨ The trading resources you need include time, financial resources, physical assets and your personal attributes.

⇨ It is highly beneficial to create a schedule for your trading to include regular times that you devote to your trading, including preparation, trading, education and review.

⇨ Consider your level of trading capital as this will influence many aspects of your trading. It is also important to consider your income needs and what level of income you wish to generate from your trading.

⇨ Physical assets for your trading include computer equipment, office furniture and an appropriate workspace.

⇨ Risk assessment is considering all the business risks that affect your ability to operate your trading business. This is *not* assessing the risk on a particular trade but the risk to being able to trade. Events you need to consider include power failure, internet failure and equipment failure.

⇨ Disaster recovery is having a plan for many of the risks that you identify in your risk assessment. Having a disaster recovery plan is a bit like having insurance— no-one wants to pay for it but they are so relieved they did when the time comes that they need it.

chapter 4

Your trading psychology

The importance of trading psychology is well known among professional traders. The impact of your trading psychology on your results is the reason we stress that you must have a personal approach to your trading. It is important to design a trading plan that will suit your personality, your personal strengths and weaknesses, and your lifestyle. In this chapter we will explore your personal strengths and weaknesses as we work toward developing a trading plan that is designed around you.

Personal attributes

It is important to evaluate your personal attributes to assess how you may react to winning or losing trades, and to provide a plan that will take advantage of your strengths and minimise the impact of your weaknesses. Your personal attributes and preferences will also determine what style of trading you will be best suited for. You are more likely to achieve success when your trading suits your natural style and requires the skills and attributes that are your natural strengths.

There are many successful traders throughout the world, each of whom has their own unique personality and trading style. When it comes to trading, there is no one formula to success — there are many roads. And that is great news for you! Whatever your personal style, there is a trading style to suit you. We have come across energetic, action-focused traders, contemplative and measured traders, and almost everything in between. However, there are some key personal attributes that are advantageous to all traders.

Discipline is a key attribute for trading. Strong discipline will ensure that you complete a trading plan and, just as importantly, you follow that plan. Completing your trading plan is not the end of the process. Don't make the mistake of putting all your time and effort into creating a great trading plan and then storing it away in the bottom drawer. Implementation of your plan needs to be an integral part of your trading at all times. Discipline is a key attribute for trading success as it ensures plans are executed and you capitalise on the work you have put in to develop the plan. Strong discipline will also ensure you review your trading results and identify weaknesses that you need to improve on and strengths that you need to build on.

Positive personal attributes

There are many personal attributes other than good discipline that contribute to successful trading. Following is a list of some of these positive attributes to get you thinking about yourself. This is not a checklist that you need to meet or a tally to see how you score. Rather it is to start you thinking about what attributes you have so that you can determine how to design a trading plan that will take advantage of your strengths.

Personal attributes that contribute to trading success include the following:

⇨ strong self-belief in your ability and trading decisions to ensure you act on your decisions and follow your trading plan

⇨ persistence and resilience to continue trading in the face of losses (which happen to every trader)

⇨ learn quickly. You enjoy acquiring new knowledge and gaining new skills

⇨ you value the time you spend on building your skills and education

⇨ disciplined nature to ensure you don't let your emotions make the decisions for you

⇨ fastidious nature. You like to keep track of progress. You are organised and focused

⇨ goal orientated. You like to set goals and track progress

⇨ you work well on your own and enjoy spending your day on the computer trading. Day trading would be a suitable option for you

⇨ you are a social person and can talk easily with others, so would get a lot of value from joining a trading group and chatting to traders online. You would not enjoy trading all day by yourself.

Tip

No matter who you are or what your background is, you will possess inherent personal attributes that will contribute to your success. Spending time to recognise and acknowledge these will build your confidence and motivation.

In the next activity, we ask you to document your positive personal attributes. We have given two examples for you. Do not let this limit your answer as you will have many more than two responses.

Activity 4.1

Think carefully about your personal attributes and how they relate to your trading. Determine your strengths and write them down. Also note down how your strengths will assist you in trading and if there is a particular style of trading you will be more suited to.

> For example: I am conservative in nature and do not act without due consideration of the issues at hand. This strength will assist me in trading as I will devote my time to developing a trading plan and then base all my decisions on this plan. I am unlikely to make emotional decisions while trading and am most likely to follow my criteria and execute my stops. Due to my more conservative and measured nature, I am more suited to a longer term trading style that allows me to assess and consider my trades without time pressure.

> Or: I have a strong desire to be successful and can focus on my goals. This gives me the determination and motivation to learn what I need to and build the skills and experience I want to be a successful trader. I will be resilient when my trades are stopped out with a loss as I have a strong belief in myself and my trading plan, and I know that this is a normal part of trading. This attribute is an asset for any trading style I decide on.

Skills and knowledge

Aside from your personal attributes, there are a range of other skills and knowledge that will contribute to your trading success. Some of these you may not have considered up until now, so this is a great process for you to recognise and affirm the skills and knowledge you already possess. In chapter 3 you listed your trading skills and knowledge. So here we want you to consider any other skills and knowledge you have that will contribute to your trading. Even as a beginner to trading, you will have skills that will contribute to your trading success. We have listed some of these skills to get you thinking about your own skills and knowledge. Once again, this is not a checklist or scorecard. This list is designed to get you thinking about what skills and knowledge you have now:

⇨ computer skills and the ability to enter data and navigate windows quickly

⇨ good general stock market knowledge, including an understanding of the data presented, derivatives available, and the process of buying and selling

⇨ good record-keeping skills

⇨ knowledge of Excel to record trades, produce graphs and calculate results

⇨ determination to follow your plans

⇨ strong visual skills—you like to see data shown in a graph and can interpret graphs quickly

⇨ good with numbers. Can interpret numbers in tables quickly and recall key numbers (key price points for particular shares) with ease.

Obviously there are many more skills and types of knowledge that could be an advantage in trading. You just need to consider your past experience and jobs that you have had to determine which skills you can capitalise on.

In the next activity, we ask you to document your skills and knowledge that you can apply to your trading. In the activity we have given two examples for you. Once again, do not let this limit your answer as you will have many more than two responses.

 Activity 4.2

Think carefully about your current skills and knowledge and how you might use these in trading. It may help you to think about your current job and what skills and knowledge you already have. You might be surprised what can be transferred over to your trading.

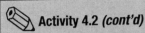 **Activity 4.2 *(cont'd)***

For example: I use a computer every day at work so I am comfortable navigating through windows, searching for information on the internet, and operating a keyboard and mouse. I know how to download software by following instructions and how to store my documents and files. All of these skills will contribute to my trading as I will be using an online broker. I can search for courses and information online, and these skills will assist me to load my software package and import the data it needs. I have also used Excel (although not extensively) so I will be able to enter my trades and I am confident I can learn to use it more proficiently as I become more familiar with it.

Or: I have always been interested in the stock market and have read many articles and books relating to trading. I am surprised at how much I do know when I talk with other people interested in the same subject. This knowledge will be advantageous in my trading as I understand many of the instruments available to trade and their advantages and disadvantages.

Not so positive personal attributes

Now that we have focused on your positive attributes, we also need to recognise what attributes you possess that may detract from your trading success. This is an important exercise to identify potential weaknesses so that your plan minimises any negative impact they may have. Alternatively, you may put in place a plan to change these attributes into more positive habits. It is possible to change your habits if you recognise what they are, determine what behaviour you want to replace this with, and then consciously practise this over and over. After a while, this will become your new habit.

Some personal attributes that may detract from trading and require management:

⇨ a tendency to procrastinate and overanalyse (afraid to enter a new trade or 'pull the trigger')

⇨ unwilling to accept losses. This is based on the false belief that if you don't sell you haven't lost any money yet. It can also be tied to a need to be right all the time

⇨ taking profits too early. Some traders like to grab hold of any profits they make and have the need to sell early when they have made an acceptable profit. If your exit strategy is based on emotion rather than analysis, it may result in missing out on potentially a much higher return

⇨ closing out too quickly with small losses. This is an emotional reaction to market movements and to protect your capital. However, this can result in increased losses if you do not allow the market enough room to move

⇨ being disorganised and not good at time management

⇨ a dislike of record-keeping or reviewing

⇨ getting easily stressed and making poor decisions under stress

⇨ risk taking—you like the excitement of living by 'the seat of your pants' and don't worry too much about planning

⇨ behaving recklessly when you have lost or made large amounts of money and start to take undue risks.

These points are by no means an exhaustive list and are only provided to start you thinking about yourself and your ability as a trader.

Tip

If you find the next exercise difficult to complete, take note of your reactions as you are trading (if you are already a trader) or try paper trading and note your reactions. What did you find natural and easy and what did you find difficult or uncomfortable?

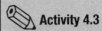 **Activity 4.3**

Think carefully about your personal attributes and how they relate to your trading. Answer the following questions about your feelings and reactions when trading. Then determine your weaknesses and develop strategies to minimise their impact on your trading.

How do you react while you are trading? Do you get excited, stressed, nervous or confident?

> For example: I get quite excited when I have entered a trade, and although I don't notice it while trading, I do notice that I relax once I have exited my position.

How do you react when you are in a losing trade? Do you get stressed, remain calm, follow your plan or get angry?

> For example: When losing trades I am very disciplined and always exit on my loss. I can get a little downcast when I have a string of losses, but generally I accept them as part of trading and a learning opportunity.

How does this affect your trading decisions?

> For example: Generally I don't feel that my emotions impact on my trading too much. However, when I have had a string of losses I lose motivation and can miss the next opportunity.

How do you react when you are in a winning trade? Do you get excited, remain calm, follow your plan or get greedy?

> For example: In winning trades I get very excited; much like watching a horse race I am urging on my position.

How does this affect your trading decisions?

> For example: I have become victim to greed and overconfidence on some occasions where I have had a big winner. This has resulted in me giving back a large part of the profits I made, believing that my trading skill had picked a great winner rather than looking for the reversal signals.

What personal attributes do you possess that you need to be aware of and improve? For each attribute you identify, note a strategy you can use to minimise its impact on your trading.

For example: I tend to be too aggressive and unwilling to accept losses. To offset any losing trades I tend to double up on the losing position to try and pick the bottom of the move and make my money back when (if?) it reverses. This usually results in making my losses even bigger when I finally accept I was wrong and exit.

Strategy: My trading strategy will always include a stop loss. I will never add to a losing position. I will spend one full week just concentrating on taking my stops in accordance with my plan and review the results.

What other factors in your life or environment affect how you trade? What strategies will you employ to minimise these?

For example: I do not make good decisions when I am tired. I will aim to treat trading as a professional job and ensure I get enough sleep before work. On days that I am tired, I will focus on reviews and research and not trade.

Your trading style

Now that you have a clear picture of your personal strengths and weaknesses, you can determine a trading style that will capitalise on your strengths and be congruent with your natural style. We would like you to consider what type of trading your personality is most suited to. For instance, are you quite aggressive and enjoy the high pace of intraday trading? Or are you more conservative, feel stressed from large swings in value of your positions and more suited to longer term time frames? Or you could be somewhere in-between and more suited to swing trading, where you have time to consider your decisions on an end-of-day basis but can look for results within a time frame of several days to several weeks. The type of trading you are most suited to (intraday, swing trader, position trader) will also be dependent upon lifestyle factors, in particular how much time you have or want to spend on trading.

It is also important to review your goals from chapter 2 at this point in time. Ensure your trading style is consistent with your overall goals and reasons for trading. This will keep you focused on achieving those goals and will give you a stronger connection between your trading activities and achievement of your goals.

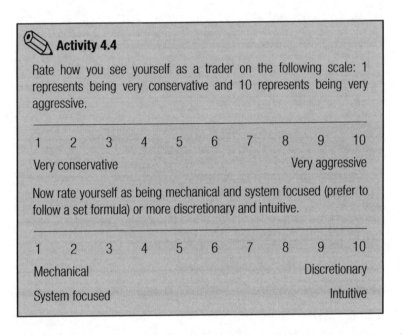

Activity 4.4

Rate how you see yourself as a trader on the following scale: 1 represents being very conservative and 10 represents being very aggressive.

1	2	3	4	5	6	7	8	9	10

Very conservative   Very aggressive

Now rate yourself as being mechanical and system focused (prefer to follow a set formula) or more discretionary and intuitive.

1	2	3	4	5	6	7	8	9	10

Mechanical   Discretionary

System focused   Intuitive

Activity 4.5

How much time do you see yourself spending on trading? All day as a full-time job? Once a day? Once a week?

Does this time frame suit your personality? (Are you a social person or do you prefer to work alone and chat online?)

Is this time frame achievable given your current financial situation and other obligations, such as work and family?

If the answer above is no, what actions can you take to rectify this?

Review your answers to activities 4.4 and 4.5. Select the trading style that best suits your personality and your time availability. Write down the key reasons you chose this style.

Long term	Medium term	Short term
Position trading	Swing trading	Day trading

For example: My trading style will be medium-term swing trading on an end-of-day basis. I will review trades each day and enter any changes to my trades or orders daily. Key reasons for this choice are:

- I still need to work full time for income.

- I like to be an active trader so would like to manage trades from a few days to a few weeks.

- I would not enjoy full-time trading by myself all day as I need more social interaction.

- I like to consider all my information and have time to analyse before reacting.

Chapter summary

⇨ Trading psychology has a significant impact on your trading results as trading is mostly about how you interact with the market.

⇨ The impact of trading psychology is the reason you need to design a trading plan that suits your personality and your particular personal attributes, strengths and weaknesses.

⇨ The best trading style is one that suits your personal style, strengths and weaknesses.

⇨ There are many personal attributes that can contribute to successful trading. Determine which personal attributes you possess (and you will have many) and what trading style is best suited to them.

⇨ You will possess a range of skills and knowledge from various aspects of your previous work and life experience that can be used in your trading. Recognising and acknowledging these will boost your confidence and motivation.

⇨ You will also possess some personal attributes that are likely to detract from your success in trading. It is important for you to recognise these attributes and plan around them.

⇨ Your challenge is to acknowledge any personal attributes that are likely to have a negative impact on your trading and either create a plan to minimise their impact or plan to modify your behaviour and create a more positive habit.

⇨ Taking note of your reactions and feelings while trading is an effective way to identify personal attributes that complement your trading and those that detract from it.

⇨ Your trading style is your level of conservatism or aggression, your level of systemisation or intuition, and your time frame.

⇨ The trading style you choose should complement your personality, capitalise on your strengths and minimise the impact of your potential weaknesses.

chapter 5

Markets, instruments and trading partners

In this chapter we will discuss some of the different trading instruments and markets that are available for you to trade. We will also look at the trading partners that you will need, including your broker, training provider, software and data providers, and other information services.

Much of the work you have done so far on assessing your current skills, knowledge and trading style will make it easy for you to decide what market and instrument you want to trade. For those who are new to trading, or even those looking to reassess their current trading, we have included a number of checklists in this chapter for assessing the trading partners and tools that you will use.

Markets and financial instruments

Now that you have established your strengths and weaknesses and the best style in which to exploit your personal attributes, you need to determine which markets and financial instruments you will trade. It is important to select markets and financial instruments that suit your trading style. For example, a conservative trader may not be suited to the highly volatile futures markets. People new to trading may be better suited to trading equities until they become familiar enough with the equities market to consider derivatives such as options or warrants.

In the following section we will discuss a number of different markets and some of the instruments that are available in each of these markets. This is certainly not a comprehensive list but more of an introductory guide for those readers who are new to trading or for traders looking for an insight into other trading opportunities they can investigate further.

Tip

When starting out trading, choose a market you are interested in and have some knowledge of. Learning is much easier when you are interested in the topic.

Equities markets

Equities are traded in most countries around the world. Equities refer to the stocks or shares issued by companies that can be bought and sold by the public through a central trading place, usually a stock exchange. There are equities that are not publicly traded; however, as you cannot trade them we will ignore them for the purposes of this discussion.

In some countries there will be one stock exchange for all company stocks (such as Australia) and in other countries there will be several stock exchanges that list different companies' stocks (such as the United States).

Equities markets are generally widely traded markets as they are easy to access and information about them is readily available. Information about the equities markets and specific company stocks is provided in the newspaper and on television, through the news and other business features. General knowledge about the stock market is higher as a result and people are more comfortable trading the stock market as an entry point.

Trading in other countries

It is possible for you to trade equities in a country outside of where you live. However, some countries do place restrictions on foreigners buying stocks, and there may be foreign taxation implications, so you will need to check these for the country you wish to trade in. Another consideration when trading stocks in another country is your exchange rate risk. This is the risk that the exchange rate will change and reduce the value of your trading account in your home currency.

What to trade

Stocks are the primary trading instrument in the equities markets for you to trade. They are generally well understood, and information about stocks and prices is readily available. However, there are a number of other financial instruments that are built around the equities market that can also be traded. Most of these are referred to as derivatives, as their price is 'derived' (or is primarily determined) from the price of the underlying stock.

Many of these are promoted to traders with limited capital as they effectively provide you with leverage. Leverage is a method by which you can expose yourself to a position in a stock (or other instrument) without having to provide the full capital amount for that position. Leverage can be obtained by trading derivatives or borrowing money. Leverage involves a higher level of risk, as a percentage move in the underlying stock will result in a larger percentage move in your capital invested. Thus your returns can be magnified but your losses can be too.

Tip

Leverage can magnify your gains—but will magnify your losses too. Leverage provides more buying power but also adds an additional level of risk to your trading.

CFDs

Contracts for difference (CFDs) are a highly leveraged financial instrument. They effectively let you trade the difference in the price of the underlying stock from the time you enter a position (open the contract) to the time you close the position (close the contract). Generally you will only need to outlay a small fraction (say, 1 per cent to 10 per cent) of the price of the underlying stock you are trading; however, the CFD price will move the same amount as the stock does. Thus you get the benefit (or cost) of the full stock price movement, but can afford to buy many more units as you only need a percentage of the stock price for each CFD you enter. These can generate large returns on your capital; however, they also carry a high degree of risk as a small negative move in the underlying stock price will have a significant negative impact on your capital.

For example, assume you wish to trade a CFD over a $50 stock and the CFD margin required for this stock is 10 per cent. This means you can enter 1000 CFDs over this stock for only $5000 (whereas 1000 shares would cost you $50 000). If the stock price moves $1 (which is a 2 per cent move), then your account balance will move $1000 (which is a 20 per cent move). So you can see the impact leveraging can have on your account—both positive and negative.

CFDs also allow you to trade long (where you profit if the stock price rises) or to trade short (where you profit if the stock price falls). When you trade short, you are effectively selling the underlying security first and buying it back later. In the case of CFDs, because they are a contract for a difference in price between two points in time, you can sell the CFD first and buy it back later.

CFDs are available as over-the-counter (OTC), where the contract you have is with a provider (usually a merchant bank), or exchange-traded, where the contract is traded publicly in the same way as stocks.

Options

Options are a contract that provides the purchaser of the option with a right (but not an obligation) to buy (a call option) or sell (a put option) a stock at a particular price. The purchaser pays the seller a premium for this right. The option contains a strike price (the price at which it can be exercised) and an expiration date, at which time the option expires and becomes worthless.

There are two types of options. An American option is an option that can be exercised anytime during its life. Thus, if the purchaser of the option wishes to exercise the option at any time up until the expiration date, the seller is obligated to either buy or sell the specified stock at the strike price. The majority of exchange-traded options are American.

A European option can only be exercised at the end of its life, at its expiration date.

Options can be used to protect the value of a current holding or to lock in a purchase price. In terms of trading, they can be used to generate income through the sale of options to collect the premiums, with the options selected being those most likely to expire worthless and hence the seller keeps the premium with no other obligation. The premium price is determined by the difference between the current price of the underlying stock and the strike price, plus an amount to allow for the time to reach expiry and risk of the underlying stock price moving in that time.

When selling options, you will be required to provide security to ensure you can meet your obligations if the purchaser of the option decides to exercise it. This security is in the form of shares in the underlying security (covered options) or cash (naked options).

Options can be over a range of financial instruments, including stocks, exchange-traded funds and stock indices.

Tip

As options are sold for a premium, they are often a great instrument for generating cash flow from trading.

Warrants

Warrants are a derivative product that allows traders to gain exposure to the underlying stock at a lower price (providing leverage in a similar way to CFDs). The warrants are issued by providers (usually merchant banks) and traded on the exchange. Like options, warrants have an exercise price and an expiry date, and they are priced in a similar fashion to options. However, unlike options, instalment warrants entitle the holder to dividends on the same date that underlying stockholders are entitled to the dividend.

Warrants have two main types. Instalment warrants are designed for medium- to long-term investors. Trading warrants can be used to trade long or short (call or put warrants) and are issued over a range of financial assets, including stocks, indices, currencies and commodities.

Margin accounts

A margin account is a good option for traders who are not comfortable trading derivatives due to their volatility and risk, but need to increase their trading capital. In a margin account, the bank will lend you funds and use the stocks that you buy as security over your loan. The amount that they will lend you will vary between stocks and is referred to as the lending ratio. A lending ratio of 60 per cent on a particular stock means that when you buy that stock in your margin account your lender will use 40 per cent of the required funds from your trading capital and lend you 60 per cent.

A margin account will provide you with the benefits of leverage, but also the risks. If the value of your stocks falls and this results in your account falling below the required lending ratio, you will incur a margin call. This will require you to deposit additional capital into your account to meet the lending ratio, or the lender will sell some of your stocks (whether you want them to or not) to make up the difference. This is nearly always at a low price as that is the reason you got the margin call in the first place.

You will pay interest on any amounts loaned to you in your margin account and need to account for this cost in your trading plan. Margin accounts can be used to purchase a range of financial instruments, including stocks, managed funds and exchange-traded funds.

Futures

Futures are contracts to buy or sell a particular asset on a specified future date at a specified price. Thus you are agreeing to buy or sell that asset at a price set today, but on a date in the future. You are speculating on where the value of that asset will be on the settlement date.

Futures can be traded short (taking the view that the value will fall below the contract value on the settlement date) or they can be traded long (taking the view that the value will be higher than the contract value on the settlement date).

You can trade a futures contract over an underlying index, commodity, currency and even interest rates. Generally the contracts will be settled in cash — the difference in the actual value and the contract value on settlement date. But this is not always the case, particularly for commodity futures, so ensure you understand the futures contract you are trading.

Futures contracts are highly leveraged. You only need to provide a small margin against the full value of the contract, but you need to ensure you can cover any margin calls if the market moves against you.

As you are speculating on a future price movement, the futures market tends to be more volatile than the underlying market. This has the advantage of creating trading opportunities.

Foreign exchange market

The foreign exchange market is for the trading of currencies. It operates 24 hours a day, five days a week. It is a highly liquid market with huge trading volumes and high levels of leverage.

You can trade the cash market, where you buy a quantity of a foreign currency at the current exchange rate by providing a margin amount, and you can close out your position at any time. Or you can trade the foreign exchange futures market, where you buy or sell a contract specifying a set exchange rate on a specified future date. Your currency futures contract will be closed out on the specified future date unless you choose to close it earlier.

Choosing your market

When choosing the market you wish to trade there are a number of factors to take into consideration. Firstly, consider what you are interested in. We spoke about the importance of passion in trading, and you will find trading a market you have an interest in far more productive and enjoyable than one in which you have little interest. It is also more likely that you will have a higher level of knowledge and understanding of a market you are interested in than one you are not.

Your trading style and personality will also influence the market you choose. Equities can be traded on many time frames, and potentially suit traders who are more conservative in their trading and have a longer time frame. Futures markets, however, are highly volatile with contracts that have set expiry dates, thus suiting a more aggressive short-term trader.

Activity 5.1

In this activity, consider your trading style, financial resources, knowledge and time frame to answer the following questions. Review your responses to previous activities on these topics if you need to.

What market do you intend to trade? Explain your choice and be specific.

> For example: I plan to trade the equities market. I am new to trading and have a conservative and measured style that will suit end-of-day trading. I am also more familiar with the stock market from my general knowledge, and need to build my trading skills for trading more volatile markets.

> Or: I have been trading stocks for several years and my plan is to expand into other markets. I am going to trade index futures as I have good trading skills and my trading style suits a fast market where I can close positions in a few hours. I can also trade the overseas futures after work a few nights a week.

What financial instruments do you intend to trade? Consider your capital requirements and if you intend to use leverage. Explain your choice.

> For example: I wish to trade stocks using a margin account, so that I can increase my current capital of $20000. I feel comfortable that I understand how a margin account works and the added risk, but believe this will be offset by the additional gains I can generate with a larger capital account to trade.

Do you need to improve your knowledge and understanding of this market or these financial instruments? How will you do this?

> For example: As I will be new to the futures market, I will open a simulation account to trade index futures to build my skills before opening a live account. I will also start reading about futures trading strategies.

Your trading tools and partners

So now that you have determined your trading style, time frame, market and instruments you wish to trade, you need to determine how you will do this. Trading requires you to use a number of service providers, or what we like to refer to as your trading partners. These providers will have a significant impact on your trading, so it is important that you are happy with their service and their prices and, if possible, that you can build a good business relationship with them.

When looking for a trading partner, the internet is a great place to start. It is always a good idea to get independent feedback on any service provider. You need to verify the marketing messages to ensure their validity. Testimonials on a website will always be glowing, or they wouldn't put them there! Talk to people at trading clubs, read trading blogs and discuss with other traders you know who have used their services. It is important to ensure that any reviews you listen to have been posted by someone who actually trades in a similar style to you and has used that particular service. Don't rely on second- or third-hand opinions.

Asking other traders for recommendations is a good place to start, but it should not be your only avenue. The service provider they recommend may be great, but it may not suit your particular style of trading in terms of the markets, financial instruments, time frame and account size. Another option for gathering information on your potential trading partners is to attend a trade show related to trading and investment, where you can visit and view the offerings of a wide variety of service providers.

The partners we will discuss in more detail are your broker, your software provider, your data provider and your training/education provider.

Tip

Always match your trading partners to your trading style, instrument and time frame.

Brokers

Your broker will be your most important business partner/ service provider for your trading business. The broker you choose will have an impact on almost every aspect of your trading, including your costs, your ease of execution, your frame of mind and your record-keeping. It is important to choose a broker who will suit your trading style and the markets you wish to trade. You may need more than one broker if you are trading different markets or different types of financial instruments.

Selecting a broker requires you to analyse and research the services available and find the one that best suits your needs. Often you will need to balance the level of service you receive with the cost you are prepared to pay. Determine what services you require and be prepared not to receive those services you are unwilling to pay for.

Consider the level of customer support you need and what service level each broker offers. This will be impacted by your current level of experience in the market, plus your familiarity with the markets you wish to trade and the platforms that the broker uses. There are a range of brokers, from full-service brokers (who advise you and enter all transactions for you) to discount internet brokers (where you do all your trade execution online), and a range of broking services that fall in between these two extremes. Consider how you want to trade and what will best meet your needs. As a general rule, the more service you want, the higher the cost. This includes how you receive support.

Brokerage fees are often what traders focus on when comparing brokers. You need to understand how each brokerage structure works and what it includes. One broker may appear to be cheaper per trade; however, they may charge you a monthly access fee as well.

Many traders sign up to a broker without reading the contract closely. It is really important that you read and understand your contract so that you know your rights and your risks. Do you know how safe your capital is? Can your broker sell your positions without your permission? What happens if the broker makes a mistake, or you have a dispute?

It is important to decide what you want from a broker. The following is a list of questions and items to consider when choosing a broker. You can use this as a checklist. Choose the brokers that will suit you and how you wish to trade first, and then look for the best deal and service level.

Checklist for evaluating a broker

⇨ Do you want to receive advice from your broker?

⇨ Will you be entering trades via the internet or over the phone?

⇨ Does the broker provide data or other market information?

⇨ Does the broker provide education or articles? Do you want these?

⇨ What is the trading platform like? Is it easy to use? Does it need to be loaded on a local PC or can you use it via the internet?

⇨ What types of orders do they offer? (For example, contingent orders and stop orders.)

⇨ How easy is it to enter orders? Amend orders? Cancel orders?

⇨ What is the brokerage structure?

⇨ What will be your brokerage costs based on how often you will trade?

⇨ Will there be additional monthly fees for data?

⇨ Will there be additional monthly fees for the online trading platform?

⇨ What types of reporting do they provide?

⇨ Can you download your trades electronically into a format such as Excel for analysis and review?

⇨ Can you readily see what trades are currently open (your portfolio) and any pending orders?

⇨ Is it a well-established company with adequate capital and equity behind it?

⇨ Where is the company based?

⇨ Is the broker easy to deal with when you enquired about their services?

⇨ What type of support does the broker provide? Email? Phone?

⇨ What hours is their support centre open?

⇨ Is the broker's call centre overseas? Does this concern you?

⇨ Who does the broker use to settle your trades (if they don't do it themselves)?

⇨ Where will your money be held? A bank account, trading account, cash management account?

⇨ Are there any fees on this account?

⇨ Does it pay interest? What rate? How often?

⇨ What markets and instruments can you trade through this broker?

⇨ Does the broker offer straight-through processing?

Checklist for margin accounts

⇨ How many shares do they offer on their approved securities list?

⇨ What margins do they offer on the types of shares you wish to trade?

⇨ What interest rate do they charge on borrowed funds?

⇨ What is the process if you receive a margin call? Do you get time to rectify the shortfall before they liquidate your position?

Selecting a CFD, forex or futures broker

As we have just discussed, it is important that you understand the contract with your broker. The structure of your contract will be partly dependent upon the type of financial instrument you will be trading. For instance, if you are trading shares, your shareholdings are held in your name and cannot be on-lent or pooled with other client holdings. If, however, you open a CFD, foreign exchange or futures account, you need to determine if your funds will be held in a separate trust account so that they cannot be used to meet the trading obligations of other clients. Under some contracts your funds will be held in a consolidated account with all other client funds and therefore will be at more risk.

Things can and do go wrong

Don't assume that you will be protected! In 2008, a broker in Australia was placed under administration. All clients who had either a short-selling or a margin account with this broker had their accounts frozen. The contracts were written in such a way that all trading accounts became assets of the broker and available to the banks as mortgagee—the trader was merely an unsecured creditor. Most lost 60 per cent of their account. Probably not what you might have expected!

Additional checklist for CFD, forex and futures brokers

⇨ Are your funds held in a separate trust account? Can your funds be used to meet obligations of other traders?

⇨ Are your funds in a consolidated account and at risk?

⇨ What backing does the provider have and is the risk acceptable to you?

Activity 5.2

Using the checklists provided in this section, note down your answers to the following questions. You may wish to revisit this activity if you have not yet determined your trading instrument or you make a change as you work through the later chapters in this book.

What market and instrument are you going to trade?

What are the key attributes you want from your broker?

Which broker are you going to use and why?

Evaluating software

Your broker will provide the platform to execute your trades; however, they may or may not provide other essential trading tools such as charting software and data feeds. In selecting your charting software and data feeds, consider your trading style and time frame to determine the level of data you need and the quality of that data. High-volume intraday futures or currency traders will require a highly accurate and timely data feed as their trading relies on accurate real-time market information. Longer term end-of-day traders will not require highly accurate intraday data. They will, however, need to consider the time at which they will receive their data, and if they need this data adjusted for company events such as share splits and dividends.

Some traders use simple charting software and utilise their own price analysis. Some traders prefer to use indicators, while others find them distracting and misleading if relied upon without further analysis. Other traders prefer to use predictive software that identifies potential trading opportunities and highlights the areas in which to enter and exit trades. Others still like to subscribe to 'tip sheets' and newsletters to provide them with trading opportunities. Regardless of what you decide to use, ensure it is in line with your trading style and provides you with value for money.

We are assuming that you will be utilising a charting package in the analysis of your trades. If you are selecting your trades on the basis of fundamental analysis only, you can apply the points in this section to the process you will use to obtain and analyse your fundamental information.

There is a huge range of different software packages in the market that provide charting for stocks and other tradeable securities. Some packages will provide charting only, while others will claim to provide secret information that will make you huge profits. The key when selecting your software is to determine what it is that you actually need to trade in accordance with your trading plan and trading style.

Tip

If something sounds too good to be true, then it probably is!

There are a huge range of indicators available in most charting packages. Whether you use them or not is your choice. It is unlikely that you will find a package that contains only the indicators you are interested in—and, besides, that may be limiting your view. You may discover as your trading progresses that there are specific indicators that you previously didn't understand or know about, which you now find quite useful. So it is great that most packages include a huge variety of indicators.

Other packages will contain the technical charts and indicators, but also complement these with other more fundamental-type information to assist your trading decisions. Some will provide alerts for certain setups and signals for entry and exit. Once again, consider how you wish to trade and choose the things that will help you.

Choosing a data supplier

Fundamental to the operation of your software will be the data it needs. Factor in the cost of data and which data providers and file formats are compatible with your software when making your selection. Depending upon your needs, there are a number of options for obtaining data. Most brokers will provide you with end-of-day data free of charge, which may be sufficient for many traders. However, you will need to obtain some historical data to create effective charts. This can be cumbersome to download if you have to do it day by day, so paying for the historical data may be a good option.

The benefits of subscribing to a data provider include the speed at which you obtain the data and the frequency of the data (intraday data by minutes, hours or ticks will definitely require a subscription). Another advantage of subscribing to data is that some data providers adjust the data to account for company events—such as dividends, bonus issues and share splits—that may distort your charts. For example, when a company issues a dividend, on the ex-dividend date the value of the price per share usually falls by an amount similar to the dividend payable. The reason for this is anyone holding the shares prior to this date is entitled to receive the dividend, whether or not they still hold the stock when the dividend is paid. However, this may not in itself affect the current price trend.

Checklist for selecting software

⇨ Is the package easy to use and navigate?

⇨ Can you find the indicators you want easily?

⇨ How do you load data into the package? Is it easy?

⇨ What providers and file formats does the package accept data from?

⇨ Can you copy, save and print your charts?

⇨ Is the editing easy to use; for example, adding your own lines and comments?

⇨ Is there an upfront fee or ongoing monthly fee, or both?

⇨ What support does it provide?

⇨ Is there an ongoing fee for licensing or support?

⇨ Is the software loaded on a local machine or on the web?

⇨ Can you load the software on multiple machines? This may be useful if you have a backup or you use a computer at home and a laptop at other times.

Checklist for selecting a data provider

⇨ What level of data do you need?

⇨ Can you receive data with a delay or do you need it in real time?

⇨ Do you receive any other information or benefits from the data provider?

⇨ Is the data provided in a number of different file formats, including one that is compatible with your software package?

⇨ Is the data adjusted for corporate events such as dividends and share splits? Do you want this?

⇨ For intraday traders, consider the speed and accuracy with which the data is provided. Some data is grouped on an intraday basis and may not be accurate if you are trying to display tick charts.

Subscriptions

Subscriptions can come in the form of 'tip sheets', where you receive specific trade recommendations, right through to newsletters on general market conditions and economic analysis. Once again, consider what it is that you will need and the value you will get from the subscription. Does the cost reflect the value you will receive?

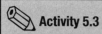 **Activity 5.3**

Using the checklists provided, note down your answers to the following questions. You may wish to revisit this activity if you have not yet determined your trading instrument or you make a change as you work through the later chapters in this book.

What are the key attributes you want from your charting software?

Which charting package are you going to use and why?

Where will you source your data and why?

> For example: I have a charting package that I like to use that provides the few indicators that I use to aid my analysis. I can get my data from my broker free of charge at the end of each trading day which is suitable for my trading style.

Do you subscribe to any other trading information, newsletters, newsfeeds or trading rooms?

> For example: I subscribe to The Speculative Investor as it is great value for money and provides me with an excellent analysis of the overall market. I prefer to complete my own filtering and analysis for trading rather than subscribe to specific recommendations.

Evaluating training providers

Finding the right training provider can be an arduous and expensive task. At Tzar Corp we have had many traders come to us with stories of having spent thousands of dollars on training courses and systems without realising the subsequent trading success they were hoping for. In many cases, these traders had failed to determine their trading style before looking to learn. As a result, they were sold into a system that sounded great but was either not as robust as the promotional material suggested or just did not suit their trading style so they had no success in applying it.

If you have worked through this book so far, you will be in the envious position of understanding your strengths and weaknesses and the trading style that is best suited to you. You now have the advantage of being able to seek out an educational course or mentor who will be suited to your style of trading and the market that you wish to trade.

The best teachers are ...

We find that the best teachers are those who are traders themselves. The reason for this is traders will have a deeper understanding of the market and a far more practical approach to their teaching than someone who just dabbles in trading or just teaches. These traders can be hard to find, and it is often difficult to determine who really does trade successfully.

As we have suggested for all your trading partners, determine what it is you want from your training provider and then do your research. Get recommendations and information on the course content from other traders who have been through the course from trading groups and trading blogs.

Checklist for selecting a training provider

⇨ Determine what you want to learn and how you want to learn before you start your search.

⇨ Research the training provider. Do they have experience trading successfully? Are they more of a trader or an educator, and which do you want?

⇨ Get feedback from course participants from independent sources (not just the testimonials on their website).

⇨ Check how the course is delivered. Is it online, in large classrooms or in small groups? What do you prefer?

⇨ What support do they offer during the course? Can you ask questions and get individual feedback on your specific trading style?

⇨ What support do they offer after the course? Is this provided by the trainers or through a call centre?

Summary

Let's take stock of all the information you have recorded so far and condense it all down to a succinct statement. Let's really define what your trading will be before we start on your trading strategies and action plan.

What you need now is a clear statement of your trading to set you on the path to achieving your trading goals. Be specific, clear and to the point. An example might be:

 Activity 5.4

My trading style is systematic and involves looking for specific trading signals. I will trade the US daytime session intraday on the futures markets using the S&P 500 E-mini contracts. I will trade through XYZ broker and utilise ABC charting software, using data from HIJ.

Using the example statement above as a guide, define your trading style, time frame, market, financial instrument, broker, software and data provider.

Chapter summary

⇨ There are many markets and many more financial instruments within these markets that you can choose to trade.

⇨ The market and financial instrument you choose to trade should be based upon your trading style, personality and level of experience.

⇨ The equities markets are the most widely understood markets and provide traders with stocks as well as a range of derivatives that can be traded.

⇨ Leverage provides you with the ability to expose yourself to a position without having to provide the full capital amount for that position.

⇨ Leverage creates more risk in trading and it magnifies the effect of any movement in the position on your level of capital. Thus it can greatly increase your return on capital, but can also magnify your losses.

⇨ Most derivatives, including CFDs, warrants and futures, provide traders with leverage.

⇨ Futures markets are highly leveraged and tend to be more volatile than the underlying market. This volatility creates trading opportunities, but due to the increased leverage and volatility these markets are generally not for beginners.

⇨ Your trading partners will include your broker, a software provider and data provider.

⇨ It is important that you select each trading partner based on your needs and your trading style.

⇨ Thoroughly research each of your providers to ensure you find the best fit for you and your personal trading style, market and time frame.

⇨ For all your trading partners, you want to be happy with their service and their price and build a good business relationship with them.

⇨ For any assets and partners you use for your trading, research them through trading clubs, blogs and talking with other traders to gain an unbiased view from someone who has had experience with them.

chapter 6

Measuring your success

In this chapter we will be looking at how to measure the success of your trading business. This encompasses both the financial side of trading and your trading statistics. We will show you how to calculate your profits, and how to calculate and interpret your trading statistics to identify ways to *increase* your trading profits.

We explain terms such as trading profit, gross profit, net profit, hit rate and edge ratio. We will also complete an exercise to determine all the operating costs for your trading business. It is important for you to understand how much you need to make to cover your expenses. Many traders just concentrate on their trading profit, without really understanding why their bank account isn't increasing at the same rate!

Determining your trading profit

We will start with the financial side of trading. This is where you calculate the profits you make from trading. Later in this chapter we will explain how to calculate and interpret your trading statistics. Your trading statistics are an essential part of assessing your trading as they will indicate areas in which you can improve in order to increase your trading profits.

Your trading profit is the gross amount that you make from each trade. It is simply the difference between the price you paid to buy the position and the price you received when you sold the position, multiplied by the number of units in that position. For a stock trade, it is the price per share you sold the shares for, less the price per share you bought them at, multiplied by the number of shares you traded.

Your trading profit is only the first part of determining the financial success of your trading. This trading profit needs to cover your direct costs of the trade plus all your other trading expenses.

Calculating gross profit

Your gross profit is your trading profit less any direct costs of the trade. In most cases, this will be your brokerage and/ or commissions charged by your broker. There may also be exchange fees charged on some futures trades that you would include in your gross profit.

When trading stocks, your gross profit will be the amount you received on the sale of your shares less what you paid for them. For the most part, your gross profit will be added directly to your trading account with your broker.

Calculating net profit

If you are calculating your gross profit from trading and making a profit, that is great! However, it is not the real profit from your trading business. You also need to deduct all your costs and expenses directly relating to your trading activities. Many traders fall into the trap of ignoring these costs as they are often met from sources other than their trading account.

For a successful trading business, you need to ensure you are making a net profit, after deducting all of your trading-related expenses. In the next section, we take you through an exercise to identify all of your trading expenses so that you can have a complete financial picture of your trading business.

Tip

The expenses related to your trading are often well hidden from your trading account. It is important to know what your monthly expenses are so you can account for them when determining the overall profitability of your trading.

Calculating expenses

It will be very tempting for you to skip over this section. In fact, we imagine many readers will skip over this entire chapter! Accounting for your trading is probably the least exciting and most tedious area of trading that you will encounter. It is one area that is often neglected by traders. However, it is important to understand the operating costs of your business—so that you don't go out of business!

Your expenses can be divided into two areas:

⇨ setup costs

⇨ ongoing expenses.

Setup costs will cover all the resources you need to start your trading business. This may include a computer, new phone line, internet setup fees, training courses and charting software. Shop around for the best deals and only buy products that are appropriate for your trading. And remember, the most expensive is not always the best.

Your ongoing expenses will usually include internet access fees, data fees, subscriptions and brokerage. Subscriptions can include magazines, online information broadcasts, electronic trading newsletters and monthly software (charting or otherwise) fees, just to name a few. If you have borrowed funds for your trading, are operating a margin lending facility or trading certain leveraged instruments, then you will also incur interest charges.

A typical monthly profit statement for your trading business could look like the following. We have used stocks as an example.

Sales of shares	5000	
Less cost of shares sold	(3000)	
Trading profit	**2000**	
Less brokerage	(100)	
Less monthly access fee	(50)	
Gross profit	**1850**	
Other expenses		
Internet fees	(80)	
Data fees	(50)	
Monthly software fee	(30)	
Subscription to investor online	(55)	
Stationery	(10)	(225)
Net profit		**1625**

 Activity 6.1

Complete the following questions to determine your setup costs and ongoing expenses.

Depending upon where you currently are with your trading, some of these questions will be merely prompts for you to think about and you will determine them after you have completed more of your detailed trading plan. For others, you may actually change some of these as you develop your trading plan.

List all your setup costs. If you already own some of these items, list them as your business assets with an approximate value.

For example: Computer, internet setup, charting software, office furniture, training.

Add up all your setup costs. This is your initial outlay for your trading business.

List all your ongoing expense items and their estimated cost.

For example: Internet, data fees, trading subscriptions, monthly brokerage fees, ongoing training, software monthly fees, news-letters, magazines.

If you currently trade or have chosen a broker, list your brokerage costs.

For example: $30 per trade up to 30 trades per month, plus $49 per month access.

Now that you have listed all your expenses it is a great idea to calculate an average monthly cost, excluding brokerage. This is the amount you need to make from your gross trading profits each month to break even. After that amount you start making clear profits.

 Activity 6.2

Using your answers to activity 6.1, calculate all your ongoing expenses as an average monthly amount. This is the amount you need to make each month before you can start counting a profit.

Trading statistics

Now that you know how to calculate your trading profit, we want to look at ways that you can analyse your trading to increase your profits. Trading statistics provide you with feedback on your trading success and identify areas on which you might focus for improvement. This is like analysing the profit margins in your business so you know where you need to improve.

Trading statistics also provide you with a means to include a financial component to your trading goals. You can use your trading statistics to identify specific actions that you can take to improve your statistics, and hence improve your overall trading profits. As we have already explained, it is far more effective to create a goal around an action or skill you can improve than to just have a financial target without a specific strategy or actions to achieve it.

The key statistics we look at are your win/loss ratio (hit rate) and your edge ratio. Other statistics that can be useful in analysing your results include your largest losing trade, largest winning trade, number of consecutive winning trades and number of consecutive losing trades.

As with all statistics, you need to have enough data in your sample to ensure it is statistically valid. Ideally, a set of at least 50 trades should be collated before calculating your statistics. This will even out unusual trades or streaks that may skew your results in a small sample of trades. However, if you are a longer term trader with a low volume of trades, a sample of 20 trades should be sufficient.

Win/loss ratio or hit rate

Your win/loss ratio is a measure of the number of times you have a winning trade as compared to your number of losing trades. We like to call this ratio your hit rate, and it represents the number of times you 'hit' a winning trade, expressed as a percentage. To calculate your win/loss ratio use the following formula:

$$\frac{\text{Number of winning trades}}{\text{Total number of trades}} \times 100 = \text{Win/loss ratio (or hit rate)}$$

The ratio is expressed as a percentage. For example, if you executed 50 trades and found that you had made a profit on

30 of them, then your win/loss ratio or hit rate would be: 30 / 50 × 100 = 60 per cent. This means for every 10 trades you enter using this particular trading strategy, on average six will be profitable and four will be losses.

Tip

A low hit rate may indicate you could improve by reviewing your entry criteria or your stop loss strategy. That is, you may be entering low-probability trades, or exiting too quickly.

Your hit rate does not determine your profitability on its own. You also need to account for the value or size of your wins and losses. This is your edge ratio.

Edge ratio

Your edge ratio is a measure of the size of your winning trades compared to the size of your losing trades. A high edge ratio will indicate that you keep your losses very small and let your winners run to large profits. A low edge ratio will indicate that the average value of your losing trades is high when compared to the average value of your winning trades.

To calculate your edge ratio, use the following formula:

$$\frac{\text{Total value of losing trades}}{\text{Number of losing trades}} = \text{Average value of losing trades}$$

$$\frac{\text{Total value of winning trades}}{\text{Number of winning trades}} = \text{Average value of winning trades}$$

$$\frac{\text{Average value of winning trades}}{\text{Average value of losing trades}} = \text{Edge ratio}$$

For example, assume that out of your 50 trades you had 30 losing trades with a total loss of $5000 and your 20 winning trades had a total profit of $10000. Your average losing trade value is $5000 / 30 = $167. Your average winning trade value is $10000 / 20 = $500. Divide the average winning trade value by the average losing trade value and you calculate your edge ratio to be 500 / 167 = 3, expressed as 3:1. This means that on average the value of your winning trades is three times higher than the value of your losing trades.

The value of your hit rate and the value of your edge ratio in isolation are of limited use when assessing if they produce a profit for you. It is the combination of the two which is important. A trader can have a profitable business with a hit rate as low as 30 per cent, as long as that trader is achieving a high enough edge ratio (in the vicinity of 4:1). Similarly, even if a trader achieves a very high hit rate, that trader can still lose money overall if he or she has very large losing trades and only small winning trades (a low edge ratio).

In the example above, we have a trader with a hit rate of 40 per cent and an edge ratio of 3:1. Using the numbers in the example above, this resulted in a profit of $5000. So even though only 40 per cent of the trades are winning trades, the overall trading is still profitable as the edge ratio is high. On the face of these statistics, you could say that this trader is good at keeping losses small and may wish to concentrate on entry criteria to improve the hit rate.

Tip

A low edge ratio may indicate that you could improve your results by setting broader profit targets or reviewing your trailing stop loss strategy.

✎ Activity 6.3

If you have already started trading, take a sample of the last 20 to 50 trades, record the profit and loss on each trade and calculate your hit rate and your edge ratio.

Total number of trades: _____

Number of winning trades: _____

Number of losing trades: _____

Total value of winning trades: _____

Total value of losing trades: _____

Average value of winning trades: _____

Average value of losing trades: _____

Hit rate: _____

Edge ratio: _____

What do these statistics tell you about your trading and what areas you might need to concentrate on?

For example: I have a high hit rate which indicates that my entry criteria are sound, but my edge ratio is low. I need to look at my stop loss strategy as my losses are too large in relation to my profits, and consider my exit strategy to try to extend my winning trades.

It is the combination of the hit rate and edge ratio that determines your profitability; these statistics need to be considered together. Your trading style will, in part, influence your trading statistics. A highly active trader may tend to have a lower hit rate by keeping losses very tight, which results in a larger edge ratio. A more conservative end-of-day trader may hold positions through large trends to achieve a very high edge ratio. So you need to consider your trading style when analysing your results. However, the absolute numbers of your hit rate and edge ratio can highlight where you might improve your results.

Other useful statistics

There are a number of other statistics that can be useful in analysing your results. These include your largest losing trade, largest winning trade, number of consecutive winning trades and number of consecutive losing trades.

Your largest losing trade and your largest winning trade can provide you with some insights into your consistency and discipline. For example, do you have one very large losing trade that brings down your overall results? This may be an indication of poor discipline in applying your stop loss, or could simply be an unusual market event that was out of your control. Recording this information as well as your trades will help you determine this. We discuss this process in chapter 7.

The number of consecutive winning trades and the number of consecutive losing trades can also provide some insight into your trading skills. In particular, consider your largest consecutive losing trades and determine if there are any factors which contributed to this. It is quite possible that this was simply a part of your trading and you had a disciplined application of your trading strategy. However, it may also indicate that perhaps you did not have the concentration or had other issues affecting your trading that you may need to address.

✎ Activity 6.4

If you have already started trading, take a sample of the last 20 to 50 trades and record the following statistics:

Largest losing trade: _____

Largest winning trade: _____

Largest number of consecutive losing trades: _____

Largest number of consecutive winning trades: _____

What do these statistics tell you about your trading and what areas you might need to concentrate on?

Chapter summary

⇨ You measure your trading success through the use of financial calculations such as trading profit and gross profit.

⇨ You use trading statistics to determine ways in which you might improve your trading profits.

⇨ Your trading profit is the gross amount you make on each trade. It is the sale value less the cost of your trades.

⇨ Your gross profit is your trading profit less your direct trading expenses, such as brokerage, commissions and monthly access fees.

⇨ Your gross profit is the amount that is usually reflected in your trading account.

⇨ It is important to understand your other expenses to ensure your gross profit from trading is covering them.

⇨ Calculating your average monthly expenses is a great tool so that you know how much you need to make each month to break even.

⇨ Your key trading statistics are your hit ratio and your edge ratio.

⇨ Your hit rate is a measure of the percentage of your trades that result in winning trades.

⇨ Your edge ratio is a measure of the relative size of your winning trades to your losing trades.

⇨ To be statistically valid, you need a sample size of between 20 and 50 trades to calculate your trading ratios.

⇨ Analysing the absolute values of your hit rate and your edge ratio can indicate how you might improve your trading results.

⇨ The values of your hit rate and your edge ratio will be influenced by your trading style.

⇨ It is the combination of the two ratios that determines your overall profitability.

chapter 7

Preparing for trading

In this chapter you are going to take stock of all the information you have collated so far and set out strategies and goals that you will target within defined time frames. A journey of one thousand miles always starts with one step. With this same philosophy, you need to have a clear focus of what you want to achieve (your thousand miles), which you have already defined in chapter 2, and then break this down into your achievable steps.

Take a moment to close your eyes and visualise your life when you have achieved the goals you set out in chapter 2. Now that you are focused on your end prize, let's break this down into achievable short-term goals (your steps) to help you get there.

Your trading goals

When setting your trading goals, it is important to focus on the skills you have, actions you can take and things you have control over. Focus on specific outcomes relating to your trading, rather than just financial goals. If you concentrate on building a robust trading strategy, consistently applying, reviewing and improving this strategy, plus building and improving your trading ability and skills, then financial rewards will surely follow. Setting a financial goal in isolation is of little value as you do not have specific actions to follow or help you to improve. Using the trading statistics we discussed in chapter 6 can help you identify specific areas in which you can improve.

Tip

Ensure your goals are specific and target areas over which you have control (such as your trading decisions and actions). Financial targets don't define actions that you can take to achieve them.

Setting your goals

Setting annual and weekly goals that are specific and orientated toward that overall goal/reward you have set for yourself is a great tool to help keep you focused and motivated. It breaks down a large task into manageable and achievable actions, and allows you to track your progress and see how you are going. In this section on setting goals you will be considering the work you have done so far in determining the areas in which you wish to improve your expertise and efficiency as a trader. We want to set goals that are quantifiable and for which you can set specific actions for achievement of those goals.

Tip

If you need to refresh the areas you identified as needing improvement, review your responses to the activities in chapter 2 and chapter 4, plus your trading statistics in chapter 6.

The time frames that you use to set your goals will, in part, be determined by the frequency and time frame of your trading. For a day trader, it will be of great benefit to set and review trading goals each week. This will keep you focused and on track and allow for continual improvement in your trading. For a longer term swing trader or position trader, perhaps monthly goal setting and review is more appropriate.

It is important to note that we talk about goal setting *and* review. It is just as important to review your achievements within a set time frame as it is to set goals. See how well you performed against your goals. This can provide you with a sense of achievement, confidence and motivation, and also highlight any areas where you might need to improve. You can also determine if you need to set new goals, extend your goals or try a new approach or strategy for the achievement of your goals.

Your annual trading goals

The place to start is to set some goals for the coming year. This can be a year from today, for the current financial year or to the end of the calendar year—whatever suits you best. Your annual goals will focus on the skills and knowledge you want to gain over this period. This may consist of learning about new markets, financial instruments and trading strategies, and implementing that new knowledge. It may be to set yourself up properly, complete your trading plan and start your trading business. You may also consider including goals relating to specific trading skills and proficiencies. Another area to consider is your personal attributes, particularly those which you have now identified as potentially impacting on your trading in a negative way.

In activity 7.1 you will set some goals for the coming annual time frame relating to knowledge, skills and personal attributes. Your goals need to be specific and targeted to defined outcomes so that you can measure your progress toward achieving them. Goals may be aimed toward improving your trading statistics, gaining certain knowledge or improving trading skills measured by adherence to your plan. These suggestions are not exhaustive and are just provided to get you thinking. For each goal, develop a strategy and/or action plan for you to achieve that goal. Determine how you will know if you have achieved each goal. The final step is your review process where you determine if you achieved your goal and need to set a new goal or wish to modify or continue with your current goal.

An example might be:

 Activity 7.1

Review the work you have done so far on identifying the areas you need to improve (in particular see activities in chapter 2 and chapter 4). Determine the goals you wish to set for the coming annual time frame. For each goal, determine a strategy and action plan for achieving that goal.

Goal: By the end of this calendar year I wish to improve my consistency in trading so that I no longer have large losses that create large drawdowns in my account.

Target area: Trading skills.

Strategy: I will set weekly goals to focus on setting and executing effective stop losses. I will record and review all my trades each week. For any week in which my losses exceed my stops by more than 10 per cent, I will set the following week's goal based around setting and executing stops.

Achievement: I will know I have achieved this goal if my equity curve is without large falls for the last four months of the year.

Review: I will review my progress at the end of this calendar year. If I achieved this goal, I will set a new goal targeting another trading skill. If not, I will review my strategy until I achieve consistency.

Tip

In completing the exercise in activity 7.1, you may wish to choose one or two goals for each area in which you indentified you needed to improve. Ensure your goals extend you but are not out of reach.

Your weekly trading goals

For each of the annual goals you set in activity 7.1, determine what actions you will take each week to move you toward achieving those goals in activity 7.2. This will break things down into specific actions and weekly reviews, which will enable you to determine when to revise and extend your weekly goals. We recommend you maintain a trading journal in which you can set your goals at the start of each week, record your trades and review your work at the end of the week. We talk more about your trading journal later in this chapter.

Note that we refer to weekly goals in this discussion. However, this short-term time frame will be entirely dependent upon your particular trading style. For a daily or intraday trader, a weekly time frame for short-term goals will be appropriate. However, for a longer term trader with less frequent trading, a fortnightly or monthly time frame may be more appropriate.

 Activity 7.2

For the purposes of this plan, set three goals for your first week, targeting the annual goals you set in activity 7.1. Each goal must be an action or achievement that brings you closer to meeting one of your annual trading goals. One of these goals may in fact be to complete this trading plan and set up your weekly trading diary.

For example:

Week commencing: 15 June

Goal no. 1: Focus on improving my record-keeping.

Activity 7.2 *(cont'd)*

Target area: Personal attribute: discipline.

Strategy 1: I will record each trade in my trading diary at the end of each day, taking note of my reasons for my trading decisions and how I was feeling about the trade.

Strategy 2: I will investigate options for automating the recording of my trades and calculation of my statistics to ease the time it takes me, so I can concentrate on strategy 1.

Achievement: I will know if I have achieved this goal if I have completed the diary and can identify improvement in my trading and see how to further improve my skills for next week. I will have also achieved this goal if I have created a process to record and calculate my statistics.

Review: I will retain this goal for two months. If I have not implemented both strategies effectively, I will retain this goal until my record-keeping has become an automatic part of my trading.

Your trading day

Now that we have a clear picture of your goals for your trading 'week', it is time to plan out your trading 'day'. We say 'day' for the purposes of this discussion; however, if you are a longer term swing or position trader, your time frame for the following tasks may be a week, a fortnight or a month.

Market prep

Before you begin trading, you need to do your market preparation (market prep). Your market prep includes an analysis of the market to date, a review of potential trading opportunities, and a review and plan for any open positions.

Market prep is an essential process to undertake before beginning any trading activity. You are trading blind if you start entering trades without having completed your market prep. You are more likely to make uninformed decisions or let your emotions affect your trading if you are not well prepared.

Your market prep should include an analysis of the market to date. This analysis may be on a number of time frames depending upon your style of trading. The analysis will include different steps depending upon what instruments you are trading. For example, if you are an intraday futures trader, your analysis will focus on the specific futures market or markets that you trade. On the other hand, if you trade stocks end of day as a position or swing trader your market prep will include review of the overall market in addition to a scan for stocks that meet your entry criteria.

Your market prep will require you to access information in addition to just your charts. In particular, you need to be aware of events that may affect the price of your current position or positions you are considering. For any market you trade, you need to know if there are significant announcements that are likely to affect the market (such as key economic data or interest rate announcements). For stocks, consider if the specific stock you are trading will have any key reporting announcements or ex-dividend dates that are likely to affect the stock price.

The second part of this activity is determining where you will get this information. A lot of this information is freely available through news reports or your broker. However, you may consider subscribing to a news service or RSS feed that will highlight the information easily for you.

In the following two sections we have outlined some market prep activities that you might undertake if you were an end-of-day stock trader or an intraday futures trader. These are designed to give you an outline that you can apply to your own personal trading style.

Stock trader market prep

For a stock trader, market prep could include the following:

1   A review of general market conditions. You should consider if there are any major news stories or events

that may impact the market as a whole. In particular, you should determine if there are any key economic data or reports due, and any key trading dates such as options expiry. Then look for any company reporting dates of positions you hold, plan to trade or for large companies that are likely to impact the sector you are trading.

2   An analysis of the daily chart of the overall market to identify key trading zones, including major and minor support and resistance areas, the current state of the market (trend or consolidation) and an assessment of the next likely direction for price movement. Include in your analysis key price zones in which you expect to see trading activity based on your analysis.

3   A scan of stocks to identify potential trading opportunities based upon your trading strategy or strategies.

4   An analysis of the daily chart for each open position and each potential trading stock to identify key trading zones, including major and minor support and resistance areas, the current state of the market for that stock (trend or consolidation) and an assessment of the next likely direction for price movement. Include in your analysis key price zones in which you expect to see trading activity based on your analysis.

Futures trader market prep

For an intraday trader on a specific market such as futures or currencies, your market prep should include:

1   A review of general market conditions. You should consider if there are any major news stories or events that may impact the market as a whole. In particular, you should determine if there are any key economic data or reports due, and any key trading dates such as options expiry.

2   An analysis of the daily chart to date to identify key trading zones, including major and minor support and resistance areas, the current state of the market (trend or consolidation) and an assessment of the next likely direction for price movement. Include in your analysis key price zones in which you expect to see trading activity based on your analysis.

3   An analysis of the previous day's intraday chart identifying the same elements on your trading time frame. This will provide you with a picture of how the market is likely to open for the current trading period.

The next step in your market prep is to consider any open positions you are holding. Review the initial trading strategy and determine if the original premise for holding these positions is still valid. Is the trade moving as you expected, or has the market changed significantly since entering so that the expectations of your trade have changed? Determine your trading strategy for these positions, in particular your exit strategy, profit target and stop loss strategy.

Tip

A great way to assess your current positions is to ask, "Would I enter this stock/position now?"

✎ **Activity 7.3**

In consideration of your trading style and time frame, determine when and how often you will perform your market preparation.

When and how often will you perform your market prep?

Outline what steps you will include in your market prep. Include how long you will spend on these steps.

How will you locate key news, trading dates and company reporting? What is your information source?

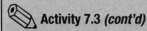 **Activity 7.3 *(cont'd)***

What is your trading plan if you identify any of the above events in your current trading session?

Will you close all positions before major announcements?

Will you trade the reaction to the announcement?

How will you scan for trading opportunities (if applicable)?

You may not yet have the answers to all of the questions outlined in activity 7.3, particularly in terms of the trading strategy you will employ in light of certain events. You can revise your answers after you have determined your trading strategy in more detail.

Daily trading record

At the end of each trading day, record all of your trading activity. As a starting point, record the details of each trade that you executed. The purpose of keeping a record of your trades is to determine how well you followed your trading plan, how well you applied your trading strategy, what you did well and what you need to work on. Also consider the trade setups that appeared that you didn't enter, and why. The purpose of this process is to look at your trading skills (rather than the trading strategy itself) and where you might be able to improve them.

Recording the facts of what happened is only part of the picture. How you were feeling and how you reacted to various situations and events are also useful to record. Consider noting down your frame of mind at the start of your trading day—were you tired, distracted or angry for other reasons, and did this affect your decision making? Also note any good luck market events or adverse market events and how you reacted to them. The more information you have the easier it will be to determine the best way to improve your trading.

For example, if an unexpected market announcement dramatically affected your position in a negative way, consider how you reacted to this event. Did you calmly assess the current position, determine a new strategy, and adjust your targets and stops accordingly? Or did you become emotional, frustrated and angry, and try to double up to get your money back? The first reaction is that of disciplined professionals who can accept the unexpected, put it behind them and continue to apply their trading plan. The second reaction can cause you to make emotional trading decisions that are likely to magnify your losses and increase your risk. This type of information in your journal will help you identify areas you need to work on to transition into a seasoned professional. This can help you determine your weekly goals and strategies to achieve them.

Your trading journal

Keeping a trading journal is an effective way to collate and record your trades as well as record all the other factors relevant to your trading. There are many different ways in which you can keep a trading journal and this needs to be something that suits you. Some traders prefer to keep their trade information in electronic format in a spreadsheet program that can automatically calculate their results. This can increase your level of accuracy and save time in working these out. If you can download your trading information directly from your broker, that is an added advantage.

The spreadsheet approach can also be useful for recording your reasons for each trade. You can record the details of each trading decision as they happen. Some traders prefer to maintain their numerical data in a spreadsheet format and keep their trading journal as a separate but complementary record. This can be as easily done in a word processing program or just written in a notebook. Other traders have software that marks their trades onto the charts as they execute and they make notes directly on the charts. It depends entirely on your personal preference. You can simply have a new page in an exercise book for each new trading day and record the other factors relating to your trading. Items you would include are your frame of mind, how you reacted to certain events and how you were feeling. It is also useful to note for each trading decision you make the key reasons for your decision. This way, you are able to more effectively assess how well you have applied your trading strategy and where you need to improve your discipline or other trading skills.

Tip

The format of your trading journal is entirely up to you. The more information you put in, the more you will get out of it.

✎ Activity 7.4

Consider keeping a trading journal. Determine your plan for recording and reviewing trades for each trading session.

How will you record and review your trades?

Will you keep a trading journal?

How often will you update your journal (as you trade, end of each day/ week)?

How long will this take?

Weekly trading review

In addition to this daily activity, allocate time for review of your overall trading week. This will include time to review the goals you set for the week and if you achieved them, calculate and review your trading statistics, review the overall progress of your trading and set new goals for the coming week. This weekly review must also be done with reference to your overall goals for trading. These goals will encompass longer term objectives that may require investment in training and skill development.

As a part of this trading review, you should consider the effectiveness of your trading strategy. However, you should only review the effectiveness of your trading strategy after you have consistently applied it over a suitable number of trades. We recommend a sample of at least 50 trades for this review; however, a smaller sample of no fewer than 20 can be used if your trading is less frequent. The key here is to ensure you have *consistently* applied your trading strategy to the trades you are reviewing. You cannot blame your strategy for poor results if you haven't in fact followed the strategy!

Another useful task is to keep a record or chart of your trading results, and in particular your trading equity. By plotting your equity regularly on a graph you will have an instant view of the success of your trading business.

Note we refer to daily and weekly tasks in this discussion. As noted earlier, if your time frame and strategy warrant, you may be better to schedule these as weekly and monthly tasks.

 Activity 7.5

Consider how you will set your short-term goals and over what time frame you will set these goals. This will be dependent upon your trading style and how often you will trade.

What is the time frame for your short-term goals?

How often will you review your progress and achievement of these goals?

When will you do this (which day of the week/month)?

How long will you spend on this review?

How often will you review the effectiveness of your trading strategy? What sample size will you use?

What amount of time will you spend on training and skill development? When?

Your trading session

Planning your trading session will ensure that you apply yourself to the task and don't fall into the trap of spending unproductive hours at your computer. Your trading session plan will outline when you will do your market prep, what hours of the day you will spend on actual trading of the market, when you will do your trading review, and the time you will devote to ongoing learning and skill development.

As we have worked through this chapter, you will have made some decisions on your time frames, when you will perform your reviews and how long you will spend on them. The purpose of activity 7.6 is to pull all of this information together into a timetable to ensure that these commitments will fit into the other obligations you have and your overall lifestyle.

 Activity 7.6

Prepare a timetable for your trading sessions (either daily or weekly). Outline your daily trading activities, including market preparation, times when you will actually execute trades and when you will record your trades. You will also need time to review your trades and note your adherence to your trading plan and the success of your trading strategy.

Free sample timetables are available at <www.tzarcorp.com> if you would like a template.

Chapter summary

⇨ Setting goals for your trading will assist you to focus on the results you want to achieve and keep you motivated.

⇨ When setting your trading goals, focus on the skills that you possess and those that you wish to improve.

⇨ Ensure your goals are specific, have a time frame and are targeted to things you can control (such as your trading decisions and actions).

⇨ The time frames in which you set your longer term goals and your shorter term goals will be dependent upon your trading style and the frequency with which you wish to trade.

⇨ For a daily trader, weekly short-term goals and a weekly review are a suitable time frame.

⇨ For a longer term trader, monthly and annual goals may be more appropriate.

⇨ Creating a timetable for all your trading activities will ensure you do not skip essential preparation and review.

⇨ A timetable will also help you to maximise the use of your time and ensure your trading suits your lifestyle and fits in with your other obligations.

⇨ Market preparation is a key activity to ensure you make informed trading decisions and have an objective view of the market. Market prep will also ensure you have a clear picture of what you want to trade and how you want to trade it.

⇨ The amount of time you spend and the tasks you undertake in your market prep will be dependent upon your trading style and the market you are trading.

⇨ Recording your trades is critical to the improvement of your trading. This record will include your trade details; however, it is beneficial to record other information such as the reasons behind your trading decisions and how you were feeling at the time.

⇨ A trading journal provides a great way to record information relevant to your trading for later review.

⇨ The more information you record, the more effective your trading review will be.

⇨ Review of your trading skills must be undertaken in addition to your review of your trading strategy.

⇨ You can only review the effectiveness of your trading strategy if you have consistently applied this strategy over a suitable number of trades.

chapter 8

Money management

In this chapter we will be focusing on how you manage the funds in your trading account. Money management encompasses determining how much of your account is put at risk for each and every trade you make. But money management is more than just determining your stop loss strategy. In this chapter we will also look at how you determine position sizing and manage both drawdowns and your increasing account balance.

The final topic we will explore in this chapter is assessing the risk of entering your selected trading opportunity. This is assessing the probability that this trade will be successful and result in a profit for you.

To discuss the topics of stop loss, risk and probability, we need to refer to a number of concepts in technical analysis. It will be useful if you have an understanding of what your trading strategy will be when working through this chapter. We recommend that you carefully read through the information in this chapter so you have an understanding of risk before starting on the next chapter in which we build your trading strategy. As you work through chapter 9, you may wish to refer back to the activities in this chapter and complete them as you are developing your trading strategy.

Trading and risk

When trading the market, there is rarely a 'right' and a 'wrong' answer. Trading is all about identifying opportunities that have the highest *probability* of moving in your direction.

Trading is all about managing risk. Selecting opportunities with limited risk and a high probability of success is what we are aiming for. No-one is ever going to trade with a 100 per cent success rate and, thankfully, that is not the aim of trading. The aim of trading is to generate a consistent and sustainable return. What we want to do as traders is ensure our losses are small and our winners are big. That's how you make money from trading. In fact, you only need to be right 50 per cent of the time and have strong trade management and you will come out with a profit.

Accepting that trading is about probabilities will also assist you in managing your emotions. You will not have an expectation that your trades will be winners 100 per cent of the time, so you become less emotional when trades are not successful and more able to execute your trading strategy effectively. As part of your money management you will have a predetermined amount that you have at risk for each trade, so you can trade with confidence and accept a string of losing trades as a part of the process. This is not to say that you should not review those trades to determine if you need to improve your execution or your strategy, but it will give you the confidence to stick to your strategy so that it can be effectively tested and reviewed at the appropriate time.

Tip

Trading is about probabilities and managing risk. You need to be comfortable that trading does not involve a 100 per cent success rate on your trades.

Determining your risk per trade

Firstly you will determine how much you will risk on each trade you enter. This is the amount you will lose if your trade is unsuccessful and you exit at your initial stop loss. This is generally done as a percentage of your trading account. You may think that risking 5 per cent of your account for each trade sounds like a reasonable risk. However, if you have 10 losing trades in a row, which is quite possible, then you have just lost 50 per cent of your total account! If you have a streak of 20 losing trades in row, which is less likely but also possible, then you have just lost your entire trading account. It is far more prudent to consider a stop loss amount that is closer to 1 per cent or 2 per cent of your total trading capital.

Activity 8.1

Determine the amount you are prepared to risk on each trade as a percentage of your total trading capital account. Also calculate this as a dollar figure.

Total trading account: _____

Percentage risk per trade: _____

Dollar value risk per trade: _____

Determining your stop loss

Your initial stop loss is the point at which you have shown that the premise for entering your trade is no longer valid and you will exit the trade. It represents the price point at which you no longer wish to be in your trade as it is now unlikely to move in the direction in which you are trading. Your initial stop loss is vital to the protection of your trading capital and will determine your level of risk per trade.

There are two main methods for determining your initial stop loss. The first is a money management stop loss. Money management stops are based on the dollar amount that you are prepared to risk on each trade. As discussed in the previous section, this is usually determined as a percentage of your trading capital. Using a money management stop you would exit the trade at the price point at which you had met the total amount you are prepared to lose on any one trade.

For example, assume your trading account balance is $10 000 and you have determined that your risk per trade will be $100 or 1 per cent of your trading capital. If you purchased 100 shares in a particular stock priced at $20 per share, then your initial stop loss would be at the price point where you were losing $100. This would be when the stock price had fallen by $1 to $19 (as $1 times 100 shares equals $100, your total risk).

The second method is based on the technical analysis of your trade. You select an exit price based on the chart pattern, so that when the price falls to your initial stop level the reason that you bought the position is no longer valid. Often this will be represented by the price breaking through the most recent technical support level or breaking a trend line.

Tip

When selecting an initial stop loss based on your technical analysis, it is often wise to choose a stop loss price slightly below the obvious support level as the price will often bounce off this point.

The scope of this book does not enable us to provide a discussion on technical analysis as the subject is vast; fortunately there are many texts available on the subject. If you are planning to use fundamental analysis only for your trade selection, then you can use a money management stop loss to manage your risk. If you are using technical chart analysis for your trade selection and management, we strongly suggest you use technical analysis to determine your initial stop loss price.

Initial stop loss and position sizing

Your initial stop loss, your risk per trade and your position size are all interrelated. If you are using a money management stop you will use the combination of your risk per trade and your position size to determine your initial stop loss point. An example of this was provided in the previous section.

If you are using technical analysis to determine your stop loss price, once you have determined your risk per trade and the price point at which you will set your initial stop loss you are in a position to determine your position size. We will step you through the process.

Assume you have already determined your money management stop or risk per trade in the previous example. The next step is completed during your analysis of each trading opportunity. This is where you determine the most appropriate price point for your initial stop loss based on your analysis of the market you are looking to enter.

Remember it is the combination of your money management and trade analysis that will help you to determine your position size. This is done using the following formula:

$$\frac{\text{Risk per trade in \$}}{(\text{Entry price} - \text{Initial stop loss price})} = \text{Position size}$$

As an example, let's say your total trading account is $50000 and you wish to risk 1 per cent per trade. Your money management risk per trade will be $500 (1 per cent × $50000). Based on your trade analysis, assume you are looking to enter a stock at $5.48 and place your initial stop loss at $5.28. In this case, you are risking 20¢ (entry price of $5.48 less stop loss price of $5.28). Your money management risk of $500 divided by your trade analysis risk of 20¢ will determine your position size to be 2500 units, or a purchase of 2500 shares totalling $13700.

Initial stop loss and leverage

If you are trading a financial instrument that provides you with leverage, ensure your calculations are based on your actual capital and not the leveraged amount. Although the leverage will enable you to trade as if you had a larger account, you still need to determine your money management risk per trade based on your actual account value (not the effective buying power of your account).

For example, if you had an account with 10:1 leverage (such as CFDs) and your account balance was $5000, this would allow you to effectively buy $50 000 worth of stock. If you calculated your risk management stop to be 1 per cent of the $50 000, this would equate to a risk of $500 per trade, representing a risk of 10 per cent of your total capital per trade!

In this case, you would need to determine your risk per trade to be 1 per cent of the $5000, or $50. Although this doesn't seem like very much, it does represent sound money management within your trading capital. If you trade with a risk of $500 per trade, you could lose half your trading capital after a string of only five losing trades.

Initial stop loss for futures and currencies

Calculating your risk for futures and currency positions is a little more complicated as you need to account for the dollar amount per point (or per pip) in your calculations. Let's say, once again, that you have a trading account of $50 000 but are now trading a futures contract which is worth $25 per point. Our money management risk of 1 per cent allows us $500 to risk per trade. After completing your trade analysis, let's say you wish to enter a trade at 8800 points and place your stop at 8795. This five-point stop equates to $125 at $25 per point. Thus, to have a total risk of no more than $500 for this trade you could buy up to four contracts ($500 / $125 = 4 contracts).

Allocation of trading funds

A second aspect to money management in trading is determining how you will allocate your funds to your trading activities. This will include allocating your trading account between different markets, different trading strategies and different trading time frames. For those traders who are just starting out or who do not have a large trading account, you will probably focus your trading on one financial market and potentially only one financial instrument. However, for those more experienced traders with larger accounts, you should make a considered decision on how your trading funds are allocated to different markets, time frames and strategies. For instance, some traders like to have an account for day trading and a separate account for a longer term outlook where they have swing trades or position trades. Further still, some traders will day trade in a futures market but hold position trades in stocks or gold or both.

It is also important to periodically review your allocation to ensure it still meets your needs or if it requires adjusting. Your trading activities will result in different levels of profit in your different accounts, therefore naturally changing your allocations. Thus it is important to periodically review your account levels to ensure they remain in line with your trading allocation plan.

 Activity 8.2

Consider your current level of experience and skill, plus your total trading account balance. Determine if you wish to concentrate your trading on one market, style and time frame or if you wish to allocate your trading funds between different markets, styles and time frames.

If you decide to allocate your funds between different trading accounts, determine how you wish to do this. Create a table of your total funds indicating market, trading style, time frame, percentage of total trading funds and dollar value. For each allocation explain your reasons.

Managing drawdowns

Even with the best laid plans it is certain that you will experience a drawdown to your trading account at some time. This may come about due to factors you can control, such as poor execution, failure to follow your plan or implementation of a flawed trading strategy. It may also come in part due to factors beyond your control, such as sudden, severe and unforeseen market movements (often reactions to news events), bankruptcy of your broker or suspension of trading by the market regulator.

You should consider that it is possible, and most probably likely, that you will experience a large drawdown in your trading account at some time during your trading career. Many traders faced with this scenario react based on their emotions—out of frustration, fear, despair or anger. A typical response to these emotions can result in traders becoming reckless and taking on undue risk to try to rectify the situation, often making it worse rather than better. If you consider that this event is likely to happen at some point in your trading career and make a plan for it, you are less likely to make poor decisions based on an emotional reaction.

You have a number of options in response to a large drawdown in your account, as listed following:

⇨ Suspend your trading to examine your trading strategy and its validity in light of your losses.

⇨ Reduce your position size to account for your reduced capital to keep your money management in place.

⇨ If a sudden market movement occurs while you have an open position, assess your position, assess the likelihood of a counter-reaction, place a new (tight!) stop and attempt to trade the counter-reaction. This should only be considered if you have the skills and experience for such a strategy.

⇨ Commit additional funds to your trading account.

Activity 8.3

Consider your plan for a large drawdown in your trading account. You may wish to have several action plans depending upon the reason for the drawdown. Determine at what value you will take your planned action.

For example: If I experience a fall in my account size of 20 per cent, I will suspend my trading to complete a detailed review of my trading strategy. I will review each of my trades to determine if I have correctly applied my strategy or need to improve my analysis and execution skills. If I determine the strategy is sound but my skills require improvement, I will invest time in my trading education before recommencing.

Or: If I enter a position and experience a significant adverse market reaction, I will create a new stop loss at a risk a quarter the size of my usual stop loss and maintain a tight trailing loss until the market corrects or I exit my position.

Managing your increasing account size

Given you are investing time and effort in developing a comprehensive plan for your trading, your chances of success have been greatly improved. As you focus on your goals and achieving them, you also need to plan for managing an increasing trading account. Determine how much you wish to have in your trading account and at what value you will withdraw funds, and plan for how you will utilise these additional funds. Do you want to use them to reward yourself? Or use as an income stream? You may wish to plan for diversifying your trading into other markets, time frames or strategies by creating a different trading account. Or you may wish to stick with your winning strategy and increase your position size.

It is important to plan for success. It is important for your self-belief, your confidence, your goals and your trading psychology. Often traders focus on minimising losses and forget to also pay attention to the profits. So take some time to plan for managing your increasing account size, be excited about the potential and have a plan for these additional funds.

 Activity 8.4

Consider your plan for your increasing trading account. Determine at what value you will withdraw funds from your trading account and what you will use them for. Also, consider if you wish to diversify your trading into other accounts and what level of funds you need to do this.

For example: I would like to increase my current trading capital from $20 000 to $30 000 before taking any money out of the account. When the account reaches $30 000, I will readjust my risk per trade based on this new capital level. Whenever the account reaches $35 000 I will withdraw $3000 (always leaving a buffer of $2000) to put toward an annual holiday with the kids.

Trade risk — assessing probability

Your trade risk is the risk that your trade will be unsuccessful and you will incur a loss as a result. You have already learned how to calculate the amount you are prepared to risk on each trade earlier in this chapter. Now we want you to consider if it is worth taking this risk. You should ask yourself: 'What is the probability that this trade will result in a loss?', and 'What reward do I receive if it is successful?'

We will consider the question of probability first. This requires you to develop a process for assessing the probability that the trade you wish to enter will be a profitable one. Essentially you need to decide if this trade has a high probability of success, or it is what we like to call a high-probability trade. There are a number of ways you can achieve this.

Firstly, you can clearly define your strategy and back-test it to see the number of times it is successful and the number of times it fails. Although this sounds easy enough, it is often very difficult to define an entry setup for back-testing and it can be an arduous process that requires programming skills.

The second approach is to determine a number of risk factors that you will assess for each trade entry you identify. You can decide that you will only enter the trade if a limited number of risk factors are present, or you may tighten your stops if you assess the risk to be higher but the trade still valid. Risk factors that you may consider include the:

⇨ size of the consolidation period before a trend starts

⇨ number of sequences completed in a trend

⇨ volatility of the price compared to recent volatility

⇨ placement of the moving average

⇨ likelihood of significant news announcements affecting this stock or market while you are holding the position.

This is by no means an exhaustive list, but is provided to stimulate your own ideas of assessing the structure of a trade in terms of risk. This assessment of risk should be outlined in each of your trading strategies (if you have more than one) as the factors you will consider will be specific to each strategy.

 Activity 8.5

What process will you use to assess the probability of your trading opportunity being profitable?

If using risk factors, list the risk factors you will use and how you will use them to assess the probability of a successful trade.

For example: When considering a potential breakout entry strategy I will assess the following risk factors:

- size of the consolidation pattern

- formation of higher lows within consolidation before the breakout

- change in volume prior to breakout

- previous overhead resistance.

I will enter the trade if no more than two risk factors are unfavourable.

Risk/reward ratio

Managing your trade risk also requires you to calculate your risk/reward ratio for each potential trade. You now have a process to determine the risk involved in your trade setup so you need to determine if, in fact, the risk is worth the potential reward. Your risk/reward ratio is calculated as the value of the profit you will make if the trade is successful in relation to the amount you will lose if your initial stop loss is hit.

For example, assume you enter a futures trade with a 20-point stop and an 80-point profit target. The ratio of profit to risk is 80/20, so the calculation would result in a risk/reward ratio of 4:1. That is, you are planning to make a profit of four times the amount you are prepared to risk on the trade.

Calculation of your risk/reward ratio will become a part of your trading process for each trade. A large risk/reward ratio, where your potential reward is significantly larger than your risk, may offset some of the risk factors you identified in the trade. The best setups are the trades with a low risk and a high risk/reward ratio. We like to call these low-risk, high-probability trades. These are the trades you want to seek out.

This risk/reward ratio will impact on your trading statistics and ultimately your trading profit. If your trades have a high risk/reward ratio, your edge ratio is likely to be higher. If your risk assessments are low, you are likely to have a higher hit rate. The higher both these ratios are, the more profit you will make.

Tip

Look for low-risk, high-probability trades. These are the trading opportunities that will make you more profitable.

Estimating your reward

Estimating your potential profit or reward on a trading opportunity can be a difficult task. There are a number of factors that you can take into consideration when estimating your potential reward. We will outline some of these factors to give you a framework in which to determine how you will estimate the reward from your trading opportunities. This is not an exhaustive list. Some of the more straightforward methods for estimating your trade's potential are:

⇨ *previous volatility*. This is where you use the size of a recent price movement to estimate the next price movement. Most often used when entering on retracements in a trend, you firstly measure the vertical distance on the previous up move in the trend. You then apply this distance to the base of the retracement to calculate your profit target.

⇨ *previous overhead resistance*. If the price action recently created a resistance zone which is currently higher than your potential entry, then the price is likely to experience some resistance at this zone again. This will create a ceiling on your potential profits in the short term. The more recent the previous overhead resistance is, the greater effect it is likely to have.

⇨ *previous price action*. When trading a breakout entry, estimating your reward can be difficult, particularly if the instrument or stock you are trading is currently making new all-time highs. You can use the most recent trend prior to the consolidation period as a guide to the potential size of the new trend. Consider if there are any factors that may impact this assumption.

Chapter summary

⇨ Trading is all about probabilities and managing your risk. Look for opportunities with low risk and a high probability of success.

⇨ Accepting that trading is about managing risk will help you to accept trading losses without emotion and execute your trades in accordance with your strategy.

⇨ It is important to determine the percentage of your trading capital you are prepared to risk on each trade; 1 per cent to 2 per cent is a good benchmark.

⇨ The amount you risk on each trade is the amount you will lose if your trade is unsuccessful.

⇨ Your initial stop loss is the price point at which your trade is no longer valid and you wish to exit. This can be determined using money management techniques or technical analysis.

⇨ Your initial stop loss, risk per trade and position size are interrelated. If trading using technical analysis, you will determine your risk per trade and initial stop loss price to calculate your position size.

⇨ If trading with leverage, determine your risk per trade based on your actual trading capital and not your leveraged amount.

⇨ Money management also requires an assessment of how you will allocate your trading capital across different markets, trading strategies and time frames.

⇨ A plan for drawdowns will assist you to continue to trade objectively and implement your actions to address the drawdown. Without a plan, drawdowns are more likely to result in emotional trading decisions that may not have the best outcomes.

⇨ You are trading to create profits, so you need a plan for your increasing account size. Be excited about the possibilities and plan what you will do with your profits.

⇨ Trade risk is assessing the probability that the trade you are considering will, in fact, result in a profit. There are a number of factors you can consider to determine how much risk is in a particular trading opportunity.

⇨ Your risk/reward ratio will calculate your possible reward as compared to the amount you are risking. You should consider your risk/reward ratio in combination with your risk assessment before entering your trade.

⇨ Low-risk, high-probability trades will provide you with the best returns.

chapter 9

Your trading strategy

All of that work and we have only just got to the fun part! If you have successfully completed the activities so far you will have a clear picture of your goals and how you will operate your trading business. You can now develop a trading strategy or strategies that will fit into your overall trading plan. Now that you understand your resources, your goals and the best way for you to trade, selection of the appropriate trading strategies will be an easy step. All of these plans so far will provide you with a sound basis for your trading for years to come. Your trading strategies, however, will develop and change as you grow as a trader.

Before we look at the steps for building your own trading strategy, we would like to discuss how indicators can be used in your strategy. We will also look at some entry and exit strategies to provide you with a framework in which to select and develop these strategies to suit your trading style. Armed with this information, you will be ready to create your own trading strategy.

Indicators and your trading strategy

There are literally thousands of indicators that you can use on your charts to assist you with your trade selection and management. Some are simple and some are complex. The thing to remember about indicators is that they are simply derivatives of price and volume. The indicator is created using a formula based upon various assumptions plus past price data and/or past volume data.

There are two points to conclude from this:

⇨ Indicators are derived from price and/or volume. They can be used effectively to support your decision-making; however, they should not replace your price analysis. It is always more accurate to work from your source data—namely the price action.

⇨ As indicators are a combination of price and/or volume, the data must have been completed in order to calculate the indicator. More often than not, the indicator will use past data between a range of time periods. As a result, indicators will always lag the price action.

Tip

Indicators can be a great tool to support your trading. However, they should not replace price analysis as your primary analysis tool.

The only indicator we would like to discuss here is the moving average and how it can be used to support your risk analysis, which was discussed in chapter 8.

Moving averages

The moving average is a line of the average closing price for a specified number of periods. It smooths out the price data and shows the trend as a line drawn on the chart. For example, on a daily chart the 30-day moving average is simply the average closing price over the last 30 days. As the moving average uses past data for its calculations, it will show a change in trend after the fact.

The longer the period used for a moving average, the smoother the line will be. As it is using older data in the calculation, it will also be slower to indicate a change in trend than a moving average based on a shorter time frame. A moving average using a short time frame (for example, 10 periods) will react quickly to a change in trend. However, it will also move more erratically.

The time period that you use will be determined by your trading time frame. If you are a longer term trader, you should use a longer period moving average in your analysis. This will provide you with signals appropriate to your time frame.

Moving averages can be used as an entry or exit signal, either using a single moving average of a combination of moving averages. We prefer to use price analysis first and use moving averages to confirm our primary conclusion.

There are two other ways in which you can use moving averages in your trading which we would like you to consider.

Confirming the state of the market

The moving average can be used as an objective way to support your analysis of a trend. If the moving average is moving up, this is supportive of an uptrend. This can be used as a supporting factor when assessing your trading opportunities.

Tip

A rising moving average does not always indicate a trend, particularly if price is ranging between two price areas. Always consider your moving average in conjunction with your price analysis.

Assessing risk

The moving average can also be used in assessing risk. You will notice on many charts experiencing an uptrend that the price will move up and then experience a retracement before continuing up again. You will see that the price moves away from the moving average during the up moves, and then moves closer to the moving average during each retracement. That is the nature of a moving average — the price will always move back toward the average after it moves away (or you can think of it as the moving average needs to move toward the price after the price has moved away).

Our conclusion from this is that the further the price is from the moving average, the greater the probability of a retracement back toward the moving average.

In our trade analysis we always look at the distance of the current price to the moving average. As the price moves further away from the moving average, we know there is an increased risk of a retracement in price back to the longer term average. Therefore, our low-risk entry points are where the price retraces back toward the moving average *and* our price analysis confirms a potential trading opportunity.

A large distance between the price and the moving average is *not* necessarily a signal to sell or a reason not to buy. It is, however, a factor to consider in your trade management and when assessing your risk/reward ratio.

Entry strategies

We will frame this discussion in the context of trading some shares for illustration purposes. We are not presenting this information as entry strategies that you can start applying. The purpose of this discussion is to look at specific factors to consider when applying your entry strategy. It is easier to illustrate some points to consider within the context of some examples.

There are two broad entry strategies that we would like to discuss briefly:

⇨ buying on the breakout

⇨ buying on a retracement.

Buying on the breakout

Buying on the breakout is where you identify a stock that is in an accumulation phase, or trading within a range of prices. You will look to enter the stock when the price breaks out above the resistance area in the expectation that an uptrend will commence. There are a number of factors to consider in this approach:

⇨ When buying on the breakout, you are taking a higher risk that this price action will form into an uptrend. The price is yet to confirm that the uptrend is in place. This price action may turn out to be a 'fake breakout' and the price falls back into the trading range or reverses direction altogether.

⇨ You are buying very early into the uptrend (if you are proven to be right), and as a result your profit potential will be higher.

⇨ After a breakout, often the price will initially retrace back to retest the original resistance zone. This may provide a secondary entry point.

Buying on a retracement

The second entry strategy we will discuss is to buy on the first retracement after the breakout. This is where you identify a stock that has broken out from a consolidation phase and has started a new trend. You are looking to enter when the first leg of the trend has made a retracement and is starting the second leg of the trend.

Some factors to consider in this approach:

⇨ Buying on a retracement carries a lower risk level for entry than buying on the breakout as you have confirmed that the uptrend is in place.

⇨ As the uptrend is now underway and the support level has held, it is more likely that you will see an advance in price in the shorter term. Thus, this approach may be more suited to a shorter term trading time frame.

⇨ Not all stocks will complete a retracement soon after the breakout. You may miss out on very profitable price moves waiting for a retracement that doesn't happen.

⇨ As you are entering at a higher price than on the breakout, your profit potential is reduced slightly. However, this is offset by your lower risk level.

It is also a valid strategy to buy on any further retracements that occur during the uptrend. It is important to ensure that the price action confirms this is a retracement (not a change in market sentiment) and the uptrend is continuing. This also provides opportunities for adding to existing winning trading positions. Be aware that the probability of an uptrend continuing will reduce as the uptrend extends.

Exit strategies

There are a number of different exit strategies that you can use, so you need to choose one that suits your particular trading style. Learning when to sell is a crucial step in your trading plan and is a skill that often takes time to develop. It is also one of the hardest areas of trading to define and often relies on your 'feel' and ability to read the market.

We categorise exit strategies into three main types:

⇨ trailing stop loss

⇨ profit-taking exit strategy

⇨ set profit targets.

Tip

You do not need to have just one of these exit strategies. It is possible to combine two of these together. For example, you can maintain a trailing stop loss at the same time as having a set profit target for exit.

Trailing stop loss

A trailing stop loss is a passive exit strategy and is a useful means of protecting your profits in a trending market. You set your initial stop loss and then move your stop to the most recent support level after each retracement in the trend. This exit strategy is only appropriate if you are trading a trend. With a trailing stop exit strategy you are exiting your position when the trend is broken.

Some factors to consider when using a trailing stop loss:

⇨ This is an effective way to protect your profits but is only appropriate if your strategy is trading with a trend.

⇨ A trailing stop loss requires the price to fall back below the last level of support, so you may be sacrificing some profits using this strategy.

⇨ This strategy can be implemented using contingent orders which will execute automatically when the price is hit. Thus it is appropriate for traders who are not actively watching their positions during the day.

⇨ It is a useful strategy to make the most from a trend, and should be considered by longer term traders, either in isolation or in conjunction with another exit strategy.

Profit-taking exit strategy

A profit-taking exit strategy is a more active exit strategy where you determine your exit based upon your real-time price analysis. Learning to read the price action in real time to determine a change in market sentiment is a skill that you will develop with experience. You need to develop a feel for the market so that you do not exit too early based on a false signal and can get the most from your winning trades.

When using a profit-taking exit strategy you are identifying a reversal signal in the price action. This may not be a complete change in trend, only the start of a retracement. Whether you are looking to trade the longer term trend or just the short-term moves within the trend depends entirely upon your time frame and trading style.

If you are trying to identify a potential change in price direction you may consider the following:

⇨ For a short-term retracement move you may look for a reversal pattern within your candlestick or bar charts such as an engulfing bar or large tails.

⇨ For a longer term change in trend you might look for a decreasing angle of ascent on the uptrend, or that the price was unable to reach a higher high, or the retracements in the trend are becoming larger and lasting longer.

We are not listing all the possibilities, only raising some areas for you to consider as you mould your own exit strategy.

The key factors to consider if using a profit-taking exit strategy:

⇨ The exit signals you are considering need to be in line with your trading time frame.

⇨ This type of strategy requires a higher level of skill and expertise than a more passive strategy. It needs to be appropriate to your level of skill and expertise.

Set profit target

A set profit target exit strategy is where you determine the price level at which you wish to exit, regardless of the actual price action. This target could be set at a specific dollar amount (for example, $500) that you want to earn from each trade, or could be a ratio to your risk or initial stop loss. Another option is to use your technical analysis to determine your set profit target, such as just below the most recent significant resistance level or a target based on previous volatility. In all cases, when your stock has risen to your specified price level, you exit.

Some factors to consider if using this exit strategy:

⇨ This is a systematic exit that can be executed automatically and is therefore suitable for a less active trader.

⇨ You may miss out on profits in two instances. If the price rises but doesn't reach your target, you will exit at your initial stop loss or hold the position as it moves between the two. You may also sacrifice profits if the trend is very strong and you exit at your target but the price action supports a much larger move.

⇨ Use of the last overhead resistance area is a sound technical analysis technique that can assist you to determine your profit target.

Creating a trading strategy

Now that we have covered some factors you can consider when determining your entry and exit strategies, we will go through each of the steps you need to follow to build your trading strategy. You should cover each of these steps for each trading strategy you use. You can apply as many trading strategies as you feel comfortable with. The key is ensuring you have an action plan for any price action that may eventuate in any strategy you implement.

Tip

The number of trading strategies you have is not an indication of your level of trading expertise. Many professional traders only have a small number of strategies that they use, but they ensure they trade them really well.

Your trading strategy will define all of your trading rules. This is where you determine which trades you will enter and how you will manage them. It should contain all the rules you need to follow for any price action that eventuates. It is the plan for the way you want to execute your trades. Having set rules for any price action that occurs in your trade will assist you to trade with sound judgement and not with emotion. You will have a rule if price goes up, a rule if price goes down and a rule if price goes sideways.

Trading is best described as executing a number of actions within an ordered process. You can think of it like a big flow chart you work through from top to bottom. At each step you have an action to undertake before moving to the next step, or you have a decision to make that will determine the next path.

By detailing all the steps required for your trading strategies you will take much of the emotion out of the trading process. It will provide a solid foundation for you to then review your trades for adherence to the strategy, and subsequently the success of that strategy. If you don't have clearly defined trading rules, you cannot assess the effectiveness of your execution or your strategy.

As we have emphasised throughout this book, it is important you implement a trading strategy that suits your particular trading style and personality. As such, it is not the purpose of this chapter to set out a trading strategy for you. There are too many markets, too many strategies and too many different trading styles for us to attempt to build a strategy that is going to suit every trader.

What we will do is provide you with a process for assessing and refining a trading strategy that will suit you. We will outline all the items to consider and provide guidance on how to assess what is best for you. This will ensure you have a structured and reasoned approach when developing your trading strategy. It is likely that you will have learned some trading strategies that you wish to apply.

You can use these as a basis for building your detailed strategy in table 9.1. Assess and mould the strategy as your work through this chapter. You will be surprised by what you can add to it based on all the knowledge you have built so far throughout this book.

Tip

A well-defined trading strategy will help you trade like a professional, with all possibilities accounted for.

Table 9.1: steps for building a strategy

Define your strategy	Have a name for your strategy and define what your trading strategy is. Briefly describe exactly what you are trading and why.
Entry criteria	How will you select your trading opportunities? What criteria are you looking for?
Filtering and selection	If you are trading stocks or a stock derivative, how will you filter stocks to determine those you will analyse?
Trade and risk analysis	What risk factors will you consider? How many risk factors will you accept and still enter the trade? Do you have different stops and position sizes for increased risk?
Initial stop loss	What is the basis for determining your initial stop loss? How will your stop be executed if hit?
Initial position size	How do you determine your position size?
Risk/reward ratio	How do you determine your profit target? Assess your risk/reward ratio for the trade.
Decision time	Based on all of the above, do you enter this trade?
Entry trigger	When you have identified potential trades for your strategy, what is the actual trigger you need to see to enter?
Re-entry	If you are stopped out of your trade, do you consider a re-entry if you criteria are still met? What conditions do you need to see to trigger a re-entry?

Table 9.1: steps for building a strategy (cont'd)

Adding	Does your strategy include adding to your winning trades?
	What conditions need to be met to do this? How much will be added? Do you have a different stop or target for the added amount?
Exit strategies	Detail how you will identify when to take profits on your trades and how much.
	Do you use a trailing stop loss? What is your process for implementing, changing and executing a trailing stop loss?
	What conditions would cause you to exit the entire position?
	Do you take some profits earlier? If so, under what conditions? How much?

As you can see, there are lots of situations that may arise for any one trade. Having a preset answer to all of these possibilities will help you to follow your plan, remain objective and trade like a professional. It is the unexpected that creates stress in trading and leads us to trade on emotions. Although it may seem like a lot of effort, once you have worked through the process a few times it will become second nature. And the rewards will be worth it.

Define your strategy

It may seem inconsequential to have a name for your strategy. However, we believe it is important to create a name and a short description that accurately describes your strategy. This will allow you to refer to your strategy by name and you will immediately turn your mind to the steps you have defined for that strategy. This is a simple technique to help you focus on your strategy and the plan you have set out for it.

Entry criteria

This is where you determine what criteria you will use to select your trading opportunities. We have briefly discussed the two main entry techniques of a breakout entry and retracement entry. Your strategy may be based on one of these, or something else. Either way, you need to define the setup you are looking for.

Tip

The more detail you have in your entry criteria, the easier it will be to find trading opportunities.

We have included a checklist below of criteria you might specify in your entry strategy for the two main strategies discussed earlier. This is presented as if you are looking to enter a stock position; however, the same factors are equally applicable for trading any market or direction.

Breakout entry

⇨ The stock price has formed a long, solid base in the accumulation phase.

⇨ The resistance area in the base was tested several times.

⇨ The price is making higher lows as it bounces off the resistance area.

⇨ Volume has increased prior to the breakout.

⇨ Wicks are appearing on the bottom of candlesticks.

⇨ There is no recent previous overhead resistance.

⇨ Price is above the moving average, which is also moving up.

Retracement entry

⇨ The up move has a steep angle of ascent.

⇨ The retracement has a shallow angle of descent.

⇨ The retracement is between 25 per cent and 50 per cent of the up move.

⇨ Wicks on the bottom of candlesticks support the start of a new up move.

⇨ Volume decreased on the retracement.

⇨ The price is not a large distance from the moving average.

Filtering and selection

Filtering and selection is only appropriate if you are trading stocks. This is the process whereby you narrow the number of stocks that you will review for your entry criteria. It is neither feasible nor efficient to try to analyse every stock in a particular market to find those that meet your entry criteria.

There are a number of ways to narrow down your selection of stocks. Some of the common methods are:

⇨ volume

⇨ industry sector analysis

⇨ market capitalisation

⇨ technical signals.

Using volume is a simple technique that will provide you with the more liquid stocks in the market. This filter is simply selecting the stocks that have traded over a certain volume during a preset period. For example, you may only consider stocks that have traded over 700 000 shares the previous day.

Industry sector analysis is a method that combines fundamental analysis into your trading. You make a considered decision that you wish to trade stocks within a particular industry sector and only search those for your entry criteria.

Market capitalisation is similar to a volume filter, whereby you only select stocks that have a market capitalisation over a certain value. This will provide you with a selection of the larger companies on that exchange.

Using technical signals as a filter requires some expertise with your charting package. This method requires you to determine certain technical signals that you wish to see and program these into your charting program. The charting program will then select those stocks for you. This can be a simple signal, such as the price closing above the open and above the moving average, or may encompass far more complicated rules. This is an effective way to narrow the range of stocks for review.

Trade and risk analysis

We covered trade and risk analysis in chapter 8. This is where you determine what risk factors you will consider that contribute to the probability of your trade setup resulting in a profit. List the risk factors that you want to consider.

In addition, determine how many risk factors you are prepared to accept and still enter the position if your entry trigger presents. An alternative approach is to plan to have a tighter initial stop loss or smaller position size if, say, more than three but fewer than five risk factors are present.

Some of the risk factors you may consider include:

⇨ a small consolidation period before a trend starts

⇨ the number of sequences completed in a trend prior to your entry

⇨ the volatility of the price compared to recent volatility

⇨ the placement of the moving average

⇨ the likelihood of significant news or market announcements affecting this stock or market while you are holding the position

⇨ the presence of recent overhead resistance.

Initial stop loss

Once again, we discussed the initial stop loss in chapter 8. For each of your trading strategies determine how you will set your initial stop loss. For example, will it be below the recent resistance or support area? If so, how far?

You also need to consider how large an initial stop loss you are prepared to accept and still enter your trade. When is it too late to enter if the risk is too large?

The final consideration in relation to your initial stop loss is determining how your stop will be executed. You may be able to enter your stop loss as a contingent order. This is where you enter your order but it is only executed if certain conditions are met. For example, a contingent stop loss may be set as:

Sell 3000 ABC at $9.15 if the price falls to $9.17.

Tip

It is often useful when trading stocks to allow yourself a little room on your contingent stop orders. If the price is moving down quickly, it may have passed your sell price when your stop is triggered and your sell may not be executed.

Initial position size

How will you determine your initial position size? This will need to be considered in conjunction with the money management risk that you have already determined in chapter 8, plus the initial stop loss price and your potential entry price. For each strategy, set out exactly how you will calculate your initial position size. You don't want to miss your entry because you can't remember how to work out how many shares or contracts to buy.

Risk/reward ratio

At this point, you need to determine what your likely return will be from this trade if it is successful. This can be difficult to determine. Factors that you can use include looking at where the most recent significant overhead resistance is, as the price is likely to experience some retracement at this point. If trading a retracement entry strategy, another option is to look at the size of the previous up move in the trend (previous volatility) and use this as a basis for estimating the next up move. If trading a breakout entry strategy, your profit target will be more difficult to estimate and you will need to look to the previous price action and volatility to guide you.

Trade analysis — decision time

After you have completed the above steps, assess the specific setup, risk factors and your risk/reward ratio to decide if you wish to enter this trade. A process for completing your trade analysis could be to set a maximum number of risk factors you will accept and a minimum risk/reward ratio.

Example trade analysis

The following trade analysis example is provided as a guide for the steps to complete for each trading opportunity you are considering. In your trade analysis you record the details that apply to the particular trade setup. It is useful to maintain a trading journal to record each trade analysis, as this will greatly assist your weekly trading reviews and identify areas to target in your goals for the following week.

This example is provided for illustration purposes only to give you a guide to the sort of information you should be recording. It is based on a fictional setup.

Name: Uptrend trading — retracement entry

Description: Entry is based on identification of a trend and entry on retracements.

Entry criteria: Looking for retracement entry where retracement is between 25 per cent and 50 per cent of the previous up move.

Filters: XYZ found—average daily stock volume 450 000, stock price $15.50.

Risk factors	Application
30-period MA	Price is above MA, MA is moving up—good
200-period MA	Price is close to 200 MA
Sequence in trend	First sequence in the trend—entering at start of second
Depth of retracement	Currently at 20 per cent of up move

Notes on risk: All risk factors are favourable at this stage. Will accept retracement of 20 per cent based on other favourable risk factors.

Watch for reversal signal for commencement of new up move, and retracement not to fall below 50 per cent of up move.

Entry trigger: Look for reversal bar such as engulfing bar forming to reversal retracement—buy on close of engulfing bar.

Initial stop loss: 1 per cent of capital = $300. Stop placed 2¢ below low of retracement.

Position size: Based on risk/(entry price – stop price)

Entry is at $15.40 and stop is at $15.28. Buy 2500.

Profit target: Profit target is 90 per cent of previous move.

Previous move of $2.45. Profit target is $17.60 ($15.40 plus 90 per cent of $2.45)

Risk/reward: Risk/reward ratio 20:1 — good.

Entry trigger

Even though you have determined your entry criteria, you still need a specific plan for exactly when you will enter the trade. It is important to specify your actual entry condition as you want the price to confirm your analysis and reason for selecting this trading opportunity. Some examples of entry triggers include:

⇨ The opening price is above yesterday's close, or a certain level above yesterday's close (the amount you decide will be determined in part by the volatility of the stock or market in question).

⇨ A reversal signal on a retracement to indicate the potential continuation of the overall trend.

⇨ The price trades at a certain level above the breakout zone.

The second step in determining your entry trigger is to consider how you will execute your entry. This may be done manually if you are watching the market, or you may need to use a contingent order.

Re-entry

Re-entry is a step that is often neglected by traders and can be the difference between a mediocre trader and a great trader. Markets do not always move in the patterns we expect or would like them to. Sometimes you will find a great trading opportunity, execute your entry and be stopped out. However, the price action may reverse back to the direction you were looking for and the trading opportunity once again presents itself. Maybe you just entered a little too early! To catch these opportunities you need to have a re-entry strategy. Set out the conditions under which you will re-enter a trade.

Tip

Don't miss out on a great trading opportunity simply because it didn't work the first time.

Adding

Adding to your positions is a more advanced trading technique that can increase your profits. After you have entered a trade and your analysis is proven to be correct, adding to your position at the right time is a low-risk strategy. You already know this is a good trade! In your trading strategy clearly define when you will add to your positions and how much you will add. You may also wish to include rules for when you will reduce your positions and by how much.

It is also perfectly fine to decide that you will not add to positions under your trading strategy. If you are not comfortable with adding, then don't do it. Your trading strategy needs to suit you.

Exit strategies

Defining your exit strategy is probably the most difficult step in setting out your trading rules. Firstly, decide what type of exit strategy, or combination of exits, you wish to apply and detail what they are. For example, you may determine that you will have a trailing stop set five cents below the support level on each retracement, but will also exit the position if you see a clear reversal signal or indication of price exhaustion. If using technical signals, clearly define what the signals are and how you will identify them.

For example, it is not sufficient to say you will exit when you see price exhaustion. Be specific and detail something like: 'Price exhaustion will be evident where a large price bar (more than twice the size of the average recent price bars) appears with either a large wick on top or is followed by a rejection bar that closes near or at its low'.

Specify if you will exit your entire position on your exit signal or will exit a set portion of your position on a technical signal and the remainder on, say, a trailing stop.

The final step in specifying your exit rules is to determine how you will execute your exit. Like your entries, this can be done manually or through a contingent order depending upon your exit rules and your trading style.

Example trading strategy

Rather than set you an activity for each of the steps for setting out your trading strategy, we have included an example following of what a trading strategy might look like. If you already have all the tools and knowledge you need to define your trading strategy and complete your trading rules, you can complete activity 9.1 now.

The following trading strategy has been provided for illustration only. Under no circumstances is it provided as a recommended or suggested trading strategy. It is simply shown to demonstrate the items you need to consider when documenting your own trading strategy.

Name: Uptrend trading—retracement entry

Description: Entry is based on identification of a trend and entry on retracements.

Entry criteria: Entry will follow identification of a consolidation pattern with a significant base, followed by a breakout and the first up move sequence in the trend. Entry will occur on the first retracement based on a reversal signal or when the price has retraced to the 30-period moving average.

Filters: Search for stocks using charting software, looking for those with more than 500 000 daily volume and value between $1 and $20 per share to identify stocks with the entry criteria.

Risk factors	Application
30-period MA	Lower risk—price is above MA, MA is moving up.
200-period MA	The closer the price is to MA on entry, the lower the risk.
Sequence in trend	Earlier in the trend sequence, lower risk (higher probability of trend continuing).
Depth of retracement	Higher risk if retracement less than 15 per cent or greater than 50 per cent of up move.

Notes on risk: If first MA is flat, or trading the third or later sequence, tighten stop to 50 per cent of strategy stop.

If large distance to 200 MA, do not enter trade.

Entry trigger: Price retracement to 30 MA. Also enter if price close to 30 MA and see reversal signal of engulfing bar or two-bar high.

Initial stop loss: 1 per cent of capital = $300.

Place stop 2¢ below lowest price on retracement if entry on reversal signal.

If enter on 30 MA, stop is placed at 50 per cent retracement level of up move.

Position size: Position size calculated to meet stop loss criteria above.

Profit target: Profit target is based on applying the distance of the previous up move to the base of the retracement.

Risk/reward: Require a risk/reward ratio of at least 3:1 to enter.

Re-entry: Re-enter on trade setup if see a reversal signal above the 50 per cent retracement level.

Adding: No adding on this strategy.

Exit strategy: Exit 50 per cent of position when at 80 per cent of profit target and see a clear reversal signal such as an engulfing bar, or at 90 per cent of profit target. Exit remaining 50 per cent when price moves into consolidation area shown by choppy action, or retracement exceeds 30 per cent on the third or later sequence in the trend.

Exit 50 per cent of position if stock price has not moved more than 20 per cent of previous volatility in 20 periods.

Exit all: Exit entire position if see a fast overextended move reaching 130 per cent of previous volatility.

 Activity 9.1

Using the example provided above (or the free online version available at <www.tzarcorp.com>), document your trading strategy by outlining each of the trading rules. Add any additional items as required to suit your individual style and strategy. Complete this exercise for each trading strategy you plan to use.

Guidelines for trading strategies

So now that you have a clear framework for setting out your detailed trading rules, we would like to discuss some general guidelines for your trading strategies.

There are many, many trading strategies that have proven to be very successful over time. So why don't they work for some traders? Most likely because traders either don't follow the strategy (maybe because they haven't properly defined their rules) or they change their strategy while they are in the trade! So in fact they are not applying the trading strategy at all. No wonder it doesn't work for them!

Never change your trading strategy mid-trade. This deprives you of the opportunity to test and improve the strategy, build your own skill level and ultimately improve your profits. If you change your strategy after entering a trade, you are not practising your strategy and building your trading skill for execution of this strategy. And, therefore, you are not learning from your trading. In fact, you are teaching yourself the worst trading mistake of all.

We have a few guidelines for trading strategies. Each of these will add enormously to your development as a trader, and as a result to your success as a trader:

⇨ Select a trading strategy that is appropriate to your trading style and time frame.

⇨ Understand your trading capital. Determine how much you want to place per trade and how many trades you want to manage at any one time.

⇨ Simple is always better. The fewer rules and parameters contained within your strategy, the easier it will be to apply.

⇨ When you start trading, select *only one* trading strategy. Practise this until you are proficient in the identification and implementation of this strategy.

⇨ Once you have mastered your trading strategy, look for ways to mould it to your particular trading style and maximise your trading edge.

⇨ Add new trading strategies to your trading plan only when you have mastered the latest one or can objectively show it is not working for you.

⇨ *Never* change your trading strategy mid-trade.

⇨ Always follow your trading rules. The best time to review the effectiveness of your trading strategy and your ability to apply the trading strategy is *after* you have exited the market.

Chapter summary

⇨ Your trading strategy will define all of your trading rules. It will determine how you identify trading opportunities, which trades you will enter and why, and how you will manage those trades.

⇨ A well-defined trading strategy and clear trading rules will help you trade like a professional. This will ensure you have an action plan for all events and do not trade based on emotions.

⇨ There are thousands of indicators you can use to support your trading decisions. Ensure you use them to support your price analysis, not replace it.

⇨ Moving averages can be used as entry or exit signals. They can also be used to help you assess the state of the market and assess your risk.

⇨ The two main entry strategies are retracement entries and breakout entries. The best entry strategy will be the one that suits your personal trading style.

⇨ There are three main exit strategies that you can use. It is possible to use a combination of exit strategies depending upon your trading style.

⇨ Building your trading strategy involves working through a framework of steps that mirrors the actions you will undertake when executing and managing your trades.

⇨ Never change your strategy mid-trade. This creates poor trading habits and robs you of the opportunity to objectively assess and review your trading skills and your trading strategy.

⇨ When you start trading, select one strategy and apply it until you have mastered it. Then you can consider adding new strategies to your trading.

⇨ Always follow your trading rules.

⇨ The best trading strategy will be the one that you design or mould to suit your particular strengths, weaknesses, level of experience and trading style.

chapter 10

Now you're ready

Congratulations! Having a trading plan is the first step to your trading success. Developing your trading strategies and implementing your plan is the next step. Remember to review your goals each week and keep these at the front of your mind.

Let's review what you have achieved so far:

⇨ You have clearly defined reasons and goals for your trading.

⇨ You have a stocktake of your trading resources and anything you need.

⇨ You have examined your skills and knowledge and any gaps you need to address.

⇨ You have been honest about your personal strengths and weaknesses and have determined strategies to effectively cater for these in your trading plan.

⇨ You understand the market and the financial instrument you want to trade and how this is appropriate for your trading style.

⇨ You know how to select and evaluate your trading partners, including your broker, training/education provider and software provider.

⇨ You understand how to determine your monthly trading expenses and calculate your net profit.

⇨ You understand the key statistics of hit rate and edge ratio and how to use these to assess your trading performance.

⇨ You know how to set your weekly goals to build your skills and expertise.

⇨ You know what to include in your market prep and why it is so important.

⇨ You have determined if you will use a trading journal and how a journal can help you to review and improve your trading.

⇨ You understand how to determine the amount you wish to risk per trade and how this is related to your initial stop loss and your position size.

⇨ You have a plan for managing drawdowns in your account and a plan to manage your profits and increasing account size.

⇨ You understand the factors you need to consider in assessing the probability of your trading opportunity being successful.

⇨ You have planned out your trading day to maximise use of your time.

⇨ You know how to apply all of the above into your trading strategies and trade execution.

Trading is as individual as each trader in the market and a personalised approach is a key to success. So it is important to develop a strategy tailor-made for you. Practise your strategy until you are proficient in both the identification of trades that fit your strategy and in the implementation of your strategy. This will take you at least 30 trades using just this one trading strategy. Once you achieve this proficiency in applying your trading strategy you will have built up the skill and experience you need to mould this strategy to your personal style.

Then you can add new trading techniques and strategies and repeat the process. With a larger range of trading strategies and trading tools at your disposal you can take advantage of a wider number of trading opportunities. As you become a more experienced trader this will become more important. You can ensure that you have strategies to apply in bull markets, bear markets and a sideways market.

Evaluation and review will be critical to building your trading expertise. So complete your trading journal for each and every trade and review it regularly. Look for areas in which you did not follow your trading strategy or trading plan. Also look for particular errors that are recurring and work on eliminating them. Include these areas with an action plan in your weekly goals.

Good luck! We wish you trading success!

Glossary

approved securities list the list of stocks that a margin lending provider will allow you to trade with leverage through a margin loan account. For each of the stocks the margin lender will indicate a leverage ratio, which shows the amount of leverage they will provide for that particular stock.

automatic stop where you enter an order to sell your current position at a set price if the price falls to a certain level. The sell is automatically triggered by your broker when the price falls to the level you have set. An automatic stop is also referred to as a contingent order.

consolidation a period in which price stops moving in a trend and commences a general sideways movement. A consolidation pattern is represented by the price moving between two price zones.

contract for difference (CFD) a highly leveraged financial instrument. CFDs effectively let you trade the difference in the price of the underlying stock from the time you enter a position (open the contract) to the time you close the position (close the contract).

contingent order an order that is entered ahead of time and executed if certain events occur, thus execution of the order is contingent on certain events. For example, a contingent order may be to buy 3000 ABC at $3.15 if the price rises to $3.14.

end-of-day trader someone who uses daily (or end-of-day) charts to make trading decisions.

ex-dividend date shareholders will be entitled to receive a dividend if they own the shares at the market close on the ex-dividend date, even if they don't own the shares on the date the dividend is paid.

intraday trader someone who buys and sells a financial instrument within one day with the purpose of generating a profit from this activity.

key price zones a range of prices at which a stock is likely to experience a high level of trading activity and potentially a change in price direction. This is equally applicable to any financial market that can be publically traded. Key price zones are often referred to as resistance areas and support areas.

personal attributes aspects of your personality and behaviour that in some way impact on your trading. Positive personal attributes include discipline, confidence, persistence and analytical skills. Negative personal attributes include impatience, recklessness, self-doubt and poor record-keeping skills.

position sizing the process of determining how many stocks, contracts or units of a particular financial instrument you will buy or sell to open a trading position.

position trader someone who buys a position for longer term growth, usually from a month to several years. The position is bought for the purposes of generating a capital gain, and may also include the generation of dividends as an ancillary purpose.

resistance zone a range of prices at which price is likely to stall or experience a change in direction and start to fall. It is a price area at which many in the market feel the stock is no longer good value and attracts selling.

risk management the process of determining how much you will lose if the position you enter does not move in the price direction you are expecting and results in a loss. Risk management also includes the process of how you will monitor these trades and execute your exit from the trade.

share splits occur when a company price per share is considered to be too high and the company proportionately increases the number of shares issued to all shareholders, resulting in a proportionate drop in the share price. For example, a company trading at $50 a share may issue every shareholder with one extra share (split all the shares into two) and this will result in the share price reducing to $25.

straight-through processing occurs when you enter a position through your online broker and the trade is automatically entered directly onto the exchange, without the broker having to enter the trade onto the exchange as a separate step.

support zone a range of prices at which price is likely to cease falling or experience a change in direction and start to rise. It is a price area at which many in the market feel the stock is now good value and attracts buying into the market.

swing trader someone who enters a position for the purpose of generating a profit over a relatively short time frame, usually from a few days to several weeks.

tick charts price charts in which the individual bars or candlesticks are represented by a preset number of underlying units traded. For example, a 30-tick chart on a futures market would show a bar or candlestick for every 30 contracts traded, regardless of the time frame in which this occurred.

trade analysis the process of reviewing and evaluating a trading opportunity or current position. This analysis could include a review of the price charts (technical analysis) and/or a fundamental analysis of the underlying stock, commodity or market.

trade management involves the ongoing review of all open trades and determining actions required based upon price changes in your position. Trade management includes determining and executing a stop loss or a trailing stop loss, adding to a position, reducing the size of a position and exiting a position.

trading the process of buying and selling to generate a profit.

trading business undertaking trading in a businesslike manner with the view to generating consistent profitability over the long term. Operating a trading business can occur over any type of market, style or trading and any trading timeframe. It is the way in which your trading is undertaken that determines your trading to be a business.

trading knowledge encompasses all the information that you have learned about trading. This will have been obtained from listening, courses and reading.

trading psychology the way in which your personal traits and your responses to different stress levels experienced while trading affect your trading decisions and actions.

trading skills the skills you gain through practise and experience entering and managing trades. These include skills such as your ability to read the market and recognise trading patterns in real time, your ability to effectively and efficiently enter and exit trades according to your trading strategy and your ability to remain focused and impartial while trading.

trading strategies the plans you have to select, enter and manage specific trading opportunities. Your trading strategy should specify how you identify a trade, how you assess the risk of the trade failing and how you will manage the trade if you enter it.

trading style the way you wish to trade, including the market you will trade, the types of trading setups you will look for, the time frame over which you plan to hold your trades and the types of strategies you will use.

trend a series of price movements in which the price is moving in a general upward or downward direction, with smaller opposite moves (retracements) along the way. A trend is generally defined in technical analysis as a series of higher high prices and higher low prices (an uptrend) or lower low prices and lower high prices (a downtrend).

Index

Printed in Australia
01 Feb 2023
LP009958

9 780730 375401